Agapanthus

for Gardeners

Agapanthus

for Gardeners

Hanneke van Dijk

TIMBER PRESS
Portland • Cambridge

Copyright © 2004 Uitgeverij Terra Lannoo BV
P. O. Box 1080, 7230 AB Warnsveld, The Netherlands

English-language edition published in 2004 by
Timber Press, Inc.
The Haseltine Building
133 S.W. Second Avenue, Suite 450
Portland, Oregon 97204-3527, U.S.A.

Timber Press
2 Station Road
Swavesey
Cambridge CB4 5QJ, U.K.

www.timberpress.com

ISBN 0-88192-656-6

Catalog records for this book are available from the Library of Congress and the British Library.

Text: Hanneke van Dijk
Design: Varwig Design, Erik de Bruin, Hengelo (The Netherlands)
Printed and bound by Proost, Turnhout (Belgium)

With thanks to the Royal Boskoop Horticultural Society

Cover photograph: *Agapanthus* 'Sylvine'
Photo page 2: *Agapanthus* 'Copenhagen'

Contents

Preface

Agapanthus is a mysterious plant that keeps you in suspense from the very moment that the flower stalk appears in the midst of the foliage. The highlight is, of course, the opening of the flowers on the inflorescence. Unfortunately, misunderstandings about this plant abound. The most notorious is that, for all kinds of obscure reasons, the plant will fail to flower, whilst we ourselves are really in control of the flowering of the plant. Certain sweeping statements have been made about the plant relative to winter hardiness. This book will put an end to all these misunderstandings.

It was high time that a book on the genus *Agapanthus* was published. Now two books have been published in cooperation with the RBHS (Royal Boskoop Horticultural Society) and the publishers Timber Press and Terra. My book, *Agapanthus: A Revision of the Genus*, is intended as a botanical reference book in which all the cultivars that are known at the present time have been described, more than 600 in all. The book *Agapanthus for Gardeners*, which you have in front of you, and which is appearing both in Dutch and English, is based on this manuscript. In this book, 80 cultivars, which have proved to be good plants both for the garden and for containers, are described. Attention has also been paid to *Agapanthus* as a cut flower.

Readers are given advice with regard to the purchase and care of the plants and, even more important, there are tips on what not to do. Hanneke and I have spent a great deal of time during the past few years e-mailing, phoning and discussing *Agapanthus*. We both hope that these wonderful plants will become even more popular than they already are.

Wim Snoeijer
Author of *Agapanthus: A Revision of the Genus*

History

A drawing of *Agapanthus africanus* by the seventeenth-century flower artist SDM, which was commissioned by the Dutch pharmacist and collector Albertus Seba

Agapanthus
The Netherlands: bloem der liefde, Afrikaanse lelie, Afrikaanse Haaklelie, Kaapse lelie, blauwe tuberroos
France: Agapanthe, Fleur d'Amour
South Africa: bloulelie, agapant, kandelaar
Great Britain: Lily of the Nile, African Lily and sometimes New African Blue Lily (1821 S. Edwards)
Germany: Afrikanische Lilie, Schmucklilie
Spain: Agapanto

The flower of love

L'Héritier was the first person to call this plant *Agapanthus*, literally translated as the flower of love. The name *Agapanthus* comes from the Greek word *agape*, which means "love", and from *anthos*, "flower". Perhaps he was acquainted with the use of this plant by the original inhabitants of South Africa: a young Xhosa bride always wears a necklace of the roots. Sometimes the whole necklace is made of dried roots; sometimes one or two pieces of root are intermingled with the beads of a necklace. A bride who has such a necklace will bear many children and give birth without complications. A young mother, who has just given birth to her first baby, will always wear such a necklace so that mother and child will be healthy and happy. The roots are also sometimes finely ground and used by the mother as a medicine prior to and after the birth. It seems that this influences the contractions of the womb. Newborns are often washed in an extract made from the flowers. The roots of the plant, which are sold at markets, are also used to heal skin complaints and to help alleviate menstrual pains. The Xhosa people also make an ointment from the roots that they use on swollen legs. The roots are only harvested in South Africa in the winter, when the plant has already set seed. Gathering them in summer is believed to cause thunderstorms. This kind of "superstition" is a form of nature conservancy, for the plants are given an opportunity to produce seed so that they can propagate before they are dug up.

V.O.C.

The English name Lily of the Nile is not exactly correct. In the first place the *Agapanthus* is not a lily and, secondly, the plant does not originate from the banks of the Nile. The Dutch name Afrikaanse lelie (African Lily) or Kaapse lelie (Cape Lily) is only half right but at least the place where it grows is correct. *Agapanthus* only occurs in the wild in one place in the world and that is South Africa. It is thus an endemic plant that does not grow in the wild outside this natural site. However, this plant has been known in Europe since the seventeenth century, thanks to the Verenigde Oost-Indische Compagnie (Dutch East India Company). In 1652 the V.O.C. set up a Dutch camp at the Cape of Good Hope. The intention was trade, but at the same time many plants found their way to The Netherlands and other countries in Europe. The Cape of Good Hope was a place of essential importance for the Company. Here they could replenish supplies before they continued on their hard voyage over the high seas. These journeys were not easy. Many sailors lost their lives, and it is by no means certain that the first *Agapanthus* taken from the country arrived alive. It was not even certain that the plants would survive in a temperate climate. The plants were, therefore, often given to botanical gardens with glasshouses, to find out which was the best way to grow such a plant.

> Good heavens! When I consider the fate of
>
> botanists then I truly doubt whether their
>
> obsession with plants is normal or insane.
>
> *Critica botanica*, Linnaeus 1737

The first *Agapanthus* was likely the evergreen *Agapanthus africanus*, and other species from the wild afterwards made their way to Europe. Almost certainly, it took some time before it was discovered that there were evergreen and deciduous species, each of which have their own specific requirements for growth. Even today this dichotomy is relatively unknown, but it must be taken into consideration.

Only in 1702 did explorers travel to more easterly situated regions of South Africa, and there they must have come across other varieties, such as *Agapanthus praecox*. In the period between 1772 and 1775 the Swede Carl Peter Thunberg (1743–1828), the Englishman Francis Masson (1741–1806) and the Swede Anders Sparmann (1748–1820) all travelled to eastern regions of South Africa. Masson was commissioned by Sir Joseph Banks of the Botanical Gardens at Kew, England, and Thunberg and Sparmann by Linnaeus. Masson and Thunberg travelled together for a time. Linnaeus (1707–1778) hated travelling himself and preferred to send his students, whom he called his apostles, to search for plants. It is highly probable that they found both *A. africanus* and another species there. In his herbarium in Uppsala there are two sheets with dried plants, one called *Mauhlia linearis* and one *A. umbellatus*. The plant that Thunberg called *Mauhlia linearis* turned out to be *A. praecox*.

Breyne

Jacob Breyne (or Breynius), a German botanist, described how he had seen a flowering *Agapanthus* in the garden of Hieronymus van Beverningk in Warmond, in The Netherlands. In 1679 he wrote in his *Prodomus Fasciculi Rariorum Plantarum*: "*Hyacinthus Africanus Tuberosus, Flore caeruleo umbellato*. This African hyacinth, which was flowering last year in the month of September in the garden of the most renowned and honoured gentleman Hieronymus Beverningk, is a remarkable wonder amongst the rare plants of Europe and it is crowned with flowers, each of which is beautiful". The name that he used translates literally as "African, tuberous hyacinth bearing umbels of blue flowers". No illustration accompanied this description; the first illustration appeared in 1739.

In 1692 the *Agapanthus africanus* was mentioned in Leonard Plukenet's *Phytographia* as *Hyacintho affinis, tuberosa radice, Africana, umbella caerulea inodora* . The latter is a new addition and means "without fragrance".

Monnincks Atlas

It is known that *Agapanthus africanus* was part of the plant collection of the Hortus Medicus in Amsterdam, in 1698. An illustration of this plant is to be found in Monnincks Atlas of 1698. Jan Monnincks (also written Monninckx and Moninx) painted plants, and one of these was *A. africanus*. The Atlas consisted of a collection of 425 watercolour and opaque watercolour illustrations. These drawings were not only made by Jan but also by Maria, who, it is presumed, was his daughter. Little is known of this family of painters from The Hague. In the same Atlas are thirteen drawings by Alida Withoos. Alida Withoos also drew flowers for Agnes Block, who grew exotic plants at her country house.

Agnes married a silk merchant from Amsterdam, Hans de Wolff, in 1649. At that time wealthy people from Amsterdam often invested their money in country estates. The de Wolff family owned a delightful country residence in Purmerend, where they spent their summers. It is assumed that they attended church in Hoorn on Sundays, so it is possible that Agnes Block met Alida Withoos, the flower artist from Hoorn, there. Presumably there were many exceptional, exotic plants at the de Wolffs' country house, and Agnes would have been very interested in them After the death of her husband, Agnes Block married another silk merchant, Sijbrand de Flines; Agnes bought her own country house at Loenen aan de Vecht, where she grew even more rare and exotic plants.

Vondel, a famous Dutch writer and also an uncle of Agnes, thought that his niece spent a great deal of her time on her plants and therefore he wrote a poem on this subject for her. The owners of these country estates often had connections with botanical gardens, and in this way the botanical garden in Amsterdam came by many special ornamental plants. They also had paintings made of the flowers. Alida Withoos was a gifted artist; she was a contemporary of Jan Monnincks, who was commissioned by Jan Commelin and Johan Huydecoper to draw "foreign plants" from the Botanical Garden in Amsterdam.

Hortus Medicus

The Hortus Medicus (Physic Garden) was set up by the municipal authorities of Amsterdam in November 1682. It was intended as a contribution towards the training of doctors and pharmacists. It was also the idea that pharmacists could buy their plants there. In cooperation with the Hortus Medicus, lessons were given in medical botany. Although the Hortus was principally for medical purposes the commissioners, Jan Commelin and Johan Huydecoper (and others later), were extremely interested in all the plants right from the start. They made use of their extensive network of country estate owners and plant collectors and, in this way, received many exceptional plants. Most important, however, were their contacts with the V.O.C. (Dutch East India Company) and the West Indische Compagnie (W.I.C.; West Indian Company). And so *Agapanthus* came to be in the Hortus Medicus in Amsterdam. During the first few years Huydecoper maintained these contacts personally, but he later advised his correspondents to send plants directly to Crommelin. The people who sent the plants to the Hortus are, for the most part, known. The name associated with *Agapanthus* is Gerbrand Pancras (1658–1716). He was mayor of Amsterdam from 1702 until 1714 and director of the V.O.C. from 1704. Moreover, he was a governor of the Hortus Medicus from 1698. The introduction of *Agapanthus africanus* in 1698 is in his name; the name given to the plant at that time was not *A. africanus* but *Hyacinthus Africanus Tuberosus, Flore caerulea*.

In 1687 one of the plants from the Botanical Garden in Leiden was listed in Hermann's catalogue. The plant was then called *Hyacintho affinis Africana Tuberosa radice umbella caerulea inodora*. Quite a mouthful for a plant but whoever translates the Latin will immediately be aware of the characteristics of the plant.

In England a flowering plant was depicted for the first time at Hampton Court Palace in 1692. It is assumed that the Dutch King Willem III, who was married to the English Princess Mary, had taken the plant to England from The Netherlands, but this is not certain.

In 1753 Heister named the plant *Tulbaghia*, and in the same year Linnaeus named the plant *Crinum africanum* whilst he also used the name *Polianthes floribus umbellatis* for the same plant. It was only in 1789 that L'Héritier, director of the Jardin des Plantes in Paris, changed the name of the plant to *Agapanthus umbellatus*. This proved to be the correct generic name, but the species was wrong (it should have been *africanus*). In 1824 the plant eventually was given its correct name when it was published by Hoffmannsegg: *A. africanus*. The wrong name, attributed to L'Heritier, *A. umbellatus*, had meanwhile started to lead a life of its own and it is, even today, sometimes erroneously used.

Marianne North

In the nineteenth century interest in exotic plants was great in the extreme. Collectors abounded and, at that time, it was also a trend for women to practise the fine arts, such as painting (there was then no possibility for women to enter a profession, but painting and travelling were accepted). In 1871 Marianne North (1830–1890), a well-to-do spinster who could paint well, went on her first world trip, which took her to the United States of America, Canada and Jamaica. Afterwards she journeyed to Brazil and, via the United States, to Japan, Borneo, Java, Ceylon and India.

By this time it was 1879, and an exceptionally successful exhibition of her paintings was held in a London gallery. The idea that her oil paintings should remain together appealed to her, so she decided to offer them to the Royal Botanical Gardens at Kew. Because there was no building at Kew large enough to accommodate her collection, which by this time was very extensive, she decided to provide a suitable building. The Marianne North Gallery was designed by James Fergusson in a style used for European houses in India. In the meantime, on the advice of her contemporary, Charles Darwin, she travelled to Australia and New Zealand and, on her return, she set about arranging her paintings in the gallery, which by then had been completed. The Marianne North Gallery was opened in 1882.

Two months later she set off for South Africa to work on more paintings, and her last two journeys were to the Seychelles and Chile. In an account of her journey to South Africa she wrote:

> It was hard work to paint all the beautiful things they brought me to Cadles. On Saturday Mr. H. telegraphed to know if I was still there and came over and spent his Sunday taking me to the head of

Postage stamp from S. Tomé, *Polianthes floribus umbellatis*, one of the names Linnaeus gave to *Agapanthus*

Van Staaden's Gorge. They gave me a perfect pony from Basutoland, a strong roan, which treated me as if I were no weight at all, and both walked and cantered to perfection. We soon reached the hills and the aqueduct leading one way to the gorge and the other to Port Elizabeth, whose streets are bordered by delicious running water, and every garden has its fountain. The gorge was very narrow and bordered by reddish cliffs, through which ran the clearest of rivers, with deep pools amid masses of ferns, pelargoniums, watsonias, blue hyacinths, yellow and white daisy trees, everlastings, polygalas, and tall heaths.

From this account it is clear that Marianne North had seen *Agapanthus*, only at that time she still called them "blue hyacinths". In a French catalogue, *Prix-Courant de Plantes Bulbeuses et Tuberculeuses* from J. Mater & Fils, Leiden, The Netherlands, from 1892–1893, ten different species and cultivars of *Agapanthus* are on offer at prices ranging from 0.15 to 1.25 cents. The prices were indicated in Dutch currency. The cheapest was *Agapanthus umbellatus*, a name that was at that time given to *A. africanus*, and the most expensive was *A. umbellatus flore pleno*, the blue, double flower that is now called *A.* 'Flore Pleno'. Thanks to the extensive botanical work of Wim Snoeijer, it has been possible to prove that not one of the ten species and cultivars mentioned retains the same name and that a number have disappeared completely.

A variable mega genus

Agapanthus has been known for centuries as a plant that belonged to large country estates. The plant was treated as a tub plant, which was put outside during the summer and kept in an orangery during the winter. Imposing tubs of *Agapanthus* stood at either side of a flight of stairs or in a courtyard. Although there has always been some movement in the assortment of available plants, the nomenclature has been sadly neglected.

A number of specialists, after thorough research, concluded that there was only one species of *Agapanthus* but that it was extremely variable. One of these was the Englishman Gordon McNeil, who wrote an article on the subject in the Journal of the Royal Horticultural Society. He travelled through Africa in January 1969 and visited several places in the region of the Katberg, where *Agapanthus* was flowering. He took notes at eleven locations and compared the length and diameter of the flowers, the length and number of the lobes, the number of flowers per inflorescence and other details. He concluded that it was indeed true that all the species and subspecies described by Frances Leighton were present but that it was just as possible that there was only one *Agapanthus* species, which was exceptionally variable. He discovered that all the populations differed enormously and intermingled and that the one species passed over into another by means of intermediaries. He acknowledged, with regard to his way of thinking, the problem of deciduous and evergreen plants. However, he believed that this could be explained by treating *Agapanthus* as a variable mega genus. And, therefore, he considered every division into species and subspecies pointless. This proposition proves once and for all that the nomenclature of the *Agapanthus* was difficult.

Mooreanus

So much for the different species; now for the cultivars. Since the seventeenth century, few true species graced European gardens. They were no longer cultivated there; many species had been grown next to each other, and the plants were propagated by seed, which resulted in hybrids.

Only at the beginning of the twentieth century was it discovered that *Agapanthus*, until then mainly considered a tub plant, could (with the necessary care, it is true) be grown in the garden. William Robinson, the great promoter of "wild gardening", mentioned *Agapanthus* in his standard work, *The English Flower Garden*. William Robinson's idea of "wild gardening" varied somewhat from what we now consider natural gardening. He saw it more as a combination of mostly exotic plants, which formed a natural garden, instead of the usual formal beds of that time, and, of course, *Agapanthus* fitted in exceptionally well.

Plants that were considered suitable for this use were called *Agapanthus mooreanus*, or *A. umbellatus Mooreanus*. Under this latter, inappropriate name, the plant received the Royal Horticultural Society's Award of Garden Merit in 1928.

Tub plant *Agapanthus* 'Whitney', one of
the Dutch Plant Collection *Agapanthus*

Agapanthus in *The English Flower
Garden* by William Robinson 1897

(1807–1879), was director of the Botanical Garden of
Glasnevin in Ireland; he was later succeeded by his son Sir
Frederick William Moore (1857–1950). Around 1890 a
German student, who worked in the Botanical Garden, sent
an *Agapanthus* to Sir Frederick Moore from South Africa,
and he called this plant *A. mooreanus*. In 1954 Lady Moore
told Lewis Palmer that she was almost certain that this plant
had come from the Orange Free State. Because of this place
of origin the plant is most probably a selection from *A. campanulatus* subsp. *patens*. But because the plant was mainly
propagated by seed right from the very beginning it would
be preferable to consider this cultivar as one group. Sir
Frederick discovered that seedlings from this plant could
survive out of doors; this was also noted in The Netherlands,
as can be seen in the *Geïllustreerd Handboek over
Bloemisterij* (Illustrated Manual for Florists), published by S.
Bleeker in 1927.

Agapanthus 'Mooreanus' is smaller and has narrow leaves
and is winter hardy when protected: the leaves then die off
in the course of the winter; new leaves appear in May, and
the flowering season is late August through September.

Lewis Palmer

Lewis Palmer received one of these abovementioned plants
shortly before the Second World War, and it survived two
cold winters in his garden in England. Whilst searching for
the origins of the plant he discovered that it was not a
species but a hybrid. He wrote in his article "Hardy
Agapanthus as a plant for the outdoor garden" that, whilst
searching, he had landed in a botanist's nomenclatural night-
mare.

Although they gave the plant the name of an evergreen
("africanus"), they wrote that the leaves of the plant died off
in winter and described the leaves as being narrower than
usual, a fact that perhaps gave rise to the fable, still believed
today, that deciduous plants have narrower leaves than evergreens. In a catalogue issued by van Tubergen in 1936, *A.
minor Mooreanus*, with narrow leaves and blue flowers on
short stems, was on offer for 35 cents for 10 plants; a year
later they were 10 cents more expensive.

This plant is now called *Agapanthus* 'Mooreanus'. The name
hails from the Moore family. The father, David Moore

Lewis Palmer's interest was aroused after his experience with *Agapanthus* 'Mooreanus' as a garden plant. Just after the war he had to go to South Africa on business, and there he visited the Botanical Garden at Kirstenbosch in Cape Town. He was shown a bed where all the wild species were growing alongside each other. He was given seed from the most beautiful of the wild species. Back home in England he continued to propagate the plants, and he introduced not only his Headbourne Hybrids but also many cultivars. It was always his intention that these were cultivars that would be able to survive outdoors in the garden, with or without winter protection.

Frances Leighton

Miss Frances M. Leighton (later Mrs. Isaac) was the first person to publish a monograph on the genus *Agapanthus*. In 1932 her attention was first drawn to *Agapanthus*, which was growing in the National Botanical Garden at Kirstenbosch in South Africa. At that time only *Agapanthus africanus, A. inapertus, A. pendulus* and *A. walshii* were known. She found that other species, such as *A. caulescens*, were described in Europe but not in their country of origin, South Africa. It was only in 1953, with the aid of the Smuts Memorial Fellowship, that she was able to make an in-depth study of the *Agapanthus* genus.

Frances M. Leighton's monograph, 'The Genus *Agapanthus* L'Héritier', was published in the Journal of South African Botany in January 1965. At that time Leighton was an assistant in the Herbarium at the University of Cape Town. The publication was in no way connected to her work, so she did it in her spare time. She built up a large collection of *Agapanthus* species at the Botanical Garden in Kirstenbosch, which originated in the wild. She discovered that the distribution of this plant was far greater than appeared from the relatively small collection in the Botanical Garden. She had always thought there were only a few species, and now she had discovered far more. She came to the conclusion that the collection in the Botanical Garden was not representative of the species but that it probably already had many hybrids. She collected 250 different plants over a period of eight years. She discovered a number herself, but most were sent to her from many parts of South Africa by botanists, profes-

sionals as well as amateurs. She concentrated on the various shapes of the flowers and the evergreen properties of the leaves.

Leighton discovered that the evergreen species originated in the southwest and southern regions of South Africa, where it rains during the winter months. The deciduous species came from more northerly areas. It intrigued her to discover that the opposite was the case with other South African monocotyledons; these latter plants grow in regions where it rains in winter if they are deciduous, whereas the evergreens occur in regions where it rains in summer. The plants in which she ascertained the difference were *Brunsvigia, Ornithogalum* and *Albuca*. In her monograph Leighton brought order into the hopelessly confused nomenclature of *Agapanthus*, determining that there were 10 species and several subspecies.

Trials

From 1971 to 1977 a trial for *Agapanthus* hybrids was held at the Royal Horticultural Society (RHS) Gardens at Wisley. A total of 71 were planted, 60 of which were from the collection of the renowned Lewis Palmer. A final conclusion was reached in 1977. These trials gave rise to a growing interest and popularity in *Agapanthus*. Unfortunately, after the report on the trials had been written and published, the plants were either done away with or planted somewhere else in the gardens, without being named. It is particularly sad, considering the beauty of the collection, that there is not a trace of Palmer's original cultivars.

In 1978, an *Agapanthus* trial was set up at the Proefstation voor de Bloemisterij (Experimental Station for Floristry), at Aalsmeer in The Netherlands. This research was carried out under the auspices of the Vakgroep Taxonomie van Cultuurgewassen (Department of Crop Taxonomy) at the Agricultural College of Higher Education, now a university, in Wageningen, The Netherlands. Fifty-eight different plants were included. In 1979 A. J. M. Gillissen conducted a study that was later published. He carried out great pioneering work in the field of classification of cultivars, distinguishing five groups and basing these groups on the shape of the flowers.

Books

Graham Duncan, well known for his knowledge of the genus *Agapanthus,* published a booklet at the National Botanical Institute, Kirstenbosch, in 1998. This booklet mainly concentrates on the various species, but general information about propagation is also given.

That same year, Wim Snoeijer, at that time working in the Department of Pharmacognosy at Leiden University, independently published a book in English, *Agapanthus: A Review*, a 256-page monograph in which all the species and 400 cultivars are described. In 2004 the standard English-language botanical work, *Agapanthus: A Revision of the Genus*, by the same author, came out. It contains descriptions of all the species (now six) and 600 cultivars. Moreover, it contains two identification keys, one for the species and one for the cultivars. This monograph brings clarity to the previous confusion in the nomenclature of the *Agapanthus*.

1679	*Hyacinthus Africanus Tuberosus, Flore caeruleo umbellato*
1687	*Hyacintho affinis Africana Tuberosa radice umbella caerulea inodora*
1692	*Hyacintho affinis, tuberosa radice, Africana, umbella caerulea inodora*
1698	*Hyacinthus Africanus Tuberosus, Flore Caerulea*
1753	*Tulbaghia – Crinum africanum – Polianthes floribus umbellatis*
1789	*Agapanthus umbellatus*
1824	*Agapanthus africanus.*

1679	*Hyacinthus Africanus Tuberosus, Flore caeruleo umbellato*

Hyacinthus (hyacinto) – is the name of a beautiful youth loved by Apollo and accidentally hit on the head and killed by Apollo during discus throwing. Apollo created a flower from the blood that flowed to the ground and bestowed upon it the name of his dead friend. According to some, this flower was a gladiolus, according to others a delphinium, and still others are of the opinion that it was the flower we now call a hyacinth.

Africanus – derived from the Latin word *Afrika*, "land of the Afri" – that again is derived from the everyday name *Afri*, "Africans" (South African Dutch)

Tuberosus – derived from the Latin word *tuber*: "tuberous"

Flore – derived from the Latin word *flos*, which means "flower"

Caerulea – Latin word meaning (dark) blue

Umbellato – derived from the Latin word *umbella* meaning "parasol" or "umbel": "joined as umbels"

1679 – African, tuber bearing hyacinth with blue flowers in an umbel.

Botany

Agapanthus at a market in Madeira

Plant description

Agapanthus is a monocotyledonous, herbaceous, perennial plant. The plants have a tuberous rootstock and fleshy, thick roots. It does not form a true root ball or tuber but has a fleshy, tuberous structure. Therefore people wonder whether this plant belongs to the bulb group or not. The plant was first named *Hyacinthus*, later on *Crinum* and *Tulbaghia*, which are all flower bulbs. The families to which *Agapanthus* was linked, the Liliaceae and the Alliaceae, were also considered bulbs. *Agapanthus* is also classed as a bulb because the bulb trade has been listing *Agapanthus* in their catalogues for over a century, and trials are regularly carried out in this branch on *Agapanthus*. At the request of the breeders, the KAVB (Royal General Bulb Growers Association) writes registration descriptions of *Agapanthus* and publishes them.

There are both deciduous plants and evergreen plants, depending upon their place of origin. If a species occurs in some wild location in Africa that is dry in winter and where there is rainfall only in summer, then it will be deciduous. In regions where it rains in winter or throughout the year, then the species will be evergreen. However, it is not the case that a deciduous plant becomes an evergreen, or vice versa, under different circumstances. Cultivars too are either evergreen or deciduous and require different conditions in their environment.

If the species are propagated in a place other than their land of origin, they will attain the same size and shape of foliage as in the wild. Even though the plant is propagated under different conditions, it will not react by adapting itself to those circumstances. However, plants obtained by division will not flower for the first few years.

Foliage

The leaves are straplike, smooth-margined, upright or arching, and generally in two rows. They have no leaf stalk, and

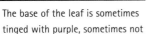

The base of the leaf is sometimes
tinged with purple, sometimes not

Peduncles with promising
flower buds protruding
above the foliage (the
Duivenvoordes)

Agapanthus bud,
surrounded by the calyx

the width varies from 1 to 5 cm. It is a myth that all plants
with wide leaves are evergreen and that all plants with narrow leaves are deciduous. The thickness of the leaves can
vary from thin to fleshy and even leathery. The position of
the leaves varies from being flat on the ground to stiffly
upright. The whole leaf or just the tips of the leaves can be
bent or arching. The colour of the leaves varies from pale to
dark green, and leaves of deciduous plants, especially, often
have a purple base. A plant forms shoots when the lateral
buds of the outer leaves sprout.

Flower

The peduncle of the plant appears amongst the leaves. This
peduncle, which protrudes above the foliage, can vary in
length from 20 to 180 cm, is either flat or round, sometimes
frosted (in other words, covered in a thin layer of wax). A
bud surrounded by a bract appears at the top of the peduncle. This paperlike bract, which often looks like a gnome's
cap, is frequently used for determination purposes. It can
open either on one side or two. Upon opening the inflorescence appears and the bract drops off. The inflorescence is an
umbel. At first sight it resembles an ordinary umbel, whereby all the small flowers grow from one central point. In real-
ity, however, the umbel is built up of helicoid cymes, each
having 3 to 10 flowers that flower one after the other. An
umbel made up of helicoid cymes, also called a bostryx, does

not occur often in the plant kingdom. The advantage is that
not all the flowers open at the same time and there are
always flowers opening on the inflorescence. *Agapanthus*
differs from *Allium*, where the inflorescence is an umbel but
it is not made up of helicoid cymes. The number of flowers
on each *Agapanthus* umbel varies immensely, depending on
the species and cultivar. There are umbels with 20 flowers
but also those with more than 100 flowers. The flower stems
vary in length from 2 to 10 cm. The flowers are upright, horizontal or nodding, depending on the species or cultivar. The
flowers are fleshy and somewhat resemble hyacinth flowers,
which is why they were originally classified with hyacinths.
The tepals are always more or less fused and are ternate.

An *Agapanthus* flower has no separate sepals and petals and,
therefore, they are called flower tepals. The base of the tepals
is fused into a flower tube. The parts of the tepals that are

Drawing from *Die Natürlichen Pflanzenfamilien*, A. Engler (1930), Verlag Wilhelm Engelsmann, Leipzig. The caption is *Agapanthus umbellatus*, but the drawing shows *A. africanus*

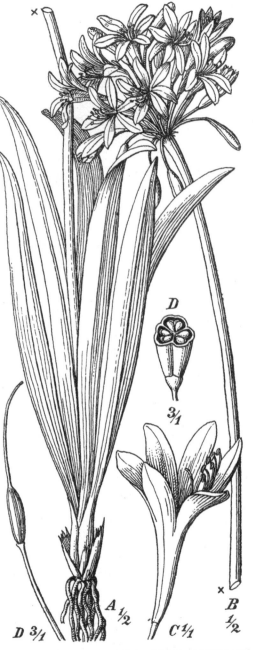

Fig. 124. *Agapanthus umbellatus* L'Hérit. *A* Blätter und Wurzel; *B* Blütenstand; *C* Einzelblüte; *D* Ovar mit Griffel; *E* Frucht im Querschnitt. (Original.)

not fused are called segments. Most flowers consist of six tepals, whereby two whorls of three are clearly visible. The tepals of the outside whorls are often longer and narrower than the inner whorl. The tepals often have a distinct midrib, differently coloured. The flower stems are slender and vary from upright to horizontal.

Each flower has six stamens that are on the tubular part of the flower. They are usually of different lengths and are sometimes exserted above the flower tepals, sometimes not. The colour of the stamens is used as a feature for identification. The pistil consists of a superior ovary with a white style and a small stigma.

The fruit is a triangular capsule, and the black, flat and winged seeds are released when the three edges of the fruit burst open. It takes about three years before a seedling flowers. The flowering season in temperate climates is usually July and August and continues through September. Cultivars are often specially selected for their early or late flowering season. The *Agapanthus* inflorescence remains attractive over a long period because, again, the buds do not all open at the same time.

Taxonomy

Many specialists have tackled the taxonomy of *Agapanthus*. The distinction of species and subspecies, the classification into a family and even the scientific name that was given to the plant has not been a matter of course. In 1679 Jacob Breyne named this plant not *Agapanthus* but *Hyacinthus Africanus Tuberosus, Flore caeruleo umbellato*. In 1687 Hermann's catalogue listed an *Agapanthus* from the Botanical Garden in Leiden as *Hyacintho affinis Africana Tuberosa radice umbella caerulea inodora*. Even Linnaeus, in 1753, did not call *Agapanthus* by this name but rather *Crinum africanum*. It was only in 1789 that the plant was given the name *Agapanthus* by L'Heritier, who was director of the Jardin des Plantes in Paris; however, he chose the wrong species name, *umbellatus*, for it should have been *africanus*. In 1824 the correct name *Agapanthus africanus* was published by Hoffmannsegg.

The fruit is a seed capsule made up of three compartments (*Agapanthus* 'Columba')

At first *Agapanthus* belonged, as a true monocotyledon, to the Liliaceae family. Later the *Agapanthus* genus was considered to be of the Alliaceae family, to which the genera *Allium*, *Nothoscordum*, *Ipheion* and *Tulbaghia* also belong. The family was subdivided, and only *Agapanthus* and *Tulbaghia* were classified as belonging to the subfamily Agapanthoideae.

Tulbaghia differs from *Agapanthus* in that the inflorescence bears far fewer flowers, the flowers are violet, green, brown or white and it smells distinctly of onions (*Agapanthus* certainly does not do this last). Taxonomists are still not in agreement as to which family *Agapanthus* should belong. Some are of the opinion that the *Agapanthus* should be classified as an Amaryllidaceae, but the plants that belong to this family have an inferior ovary whereas *Agapanthus* has a superior ovary. Hutchinson, who classified *Agapanthus* as belonging to the Amaryllidaceae, believed that the umbel-shaped inflorescence was of more importance than whether the plant had a superior or inferior ovary.

In 1998 Wim Snoeijer concluded that *Agapanthus* would best be classed in a family of its own, Agapanthaceae, to which only the genus *Agapanthus* should belong. Nowadays this opinion is shared by most taxonomists.

From ten species to six

Frances M. Leighton's authoritative 1965 monograph, 'The Genus *Agapanthus* L'Héritier', was considered for many years the last word on the subject. In it, she distinguished ten species (and the requisite subspecies and varieties, which are not mentioned here):

A. campanulatus
A. caulescens
A. coddii
A. praecox
A. inapertus
A. africanus
A. comptonii
A. walshii
A. dyeri
A. nutans

According to Zonneveld and Duncan, following DNA research, there are in 2003 only six species left; the other four are either synonyms or subspecies. Only the subspecies (subsp.) are mentioned here:

A. campanulatus
A. caulescens (including *A. nutans*)
A. coddii
A. praecox
    A. praecox subsp. *minimus* (including *A. comptonii*)
A. inapertus
    A. inapertus subsp. *intermedius* (including *A. dyeri*)
A. africanus
    A. africanus subsp. *walshii* (was *A. walshii*)

Agapanthus praecox and *A. africanus* and their subspecies are evergreen; *A. campanulatus, A. caulescens, A. coddii* and *A. inapertus* are deciduous.

Zonneveld and Duncan (2003) suggested a botanical classification for the six species of two sections. This division is based on the colour of the pollen and the DNA content:

Section Lilacinipollini
A. campanulatus
A. caulescens
A. coddii
All three species have purple pollen and are deciduous; the leaves are purple at the base.

Section Ochraceipollini
A. africanus
A. inapertus
A. praecox
These three species have yellow pollen and are either deciduous or evergreen; the leaves have a green or purple base.

Classification of the cultivars

This classification of the cultivars is based mainly on the proposal made by Gillissen in the report he wrote following his MA research at the University for Agriculture, Wageningen, in 1980. Gillissen based the classification on the shape of the flower and whether the plant is evergreen or deciduous. He classified the cultivars into five groups, related to the species: Praecox Group, Africanus Group, Intermediate Group, Campanulatus Group and Inapertus Group.

Snoeijer (1998) used only four instead of five groups, leaving the Intermediate Group aside; and in *Agapanthus: A Revision of the Genus* (2004) he changed the names of the groups: they are now based on the shape of the flower instead of the species. The Praecox Group became the Funnel Group, the Africanus Group the Trumpet Group, the Campanulatus Group the Salver Group and the Inapertus Group the Tubular Group. The advantage is that a cultivar is not immediately associated with a species, as a result of which specialists often tended to attach other, often inapplicable, characteristics to the plants. The classification of the cultivars in four groups has, on the advice of Marco Hoffman, been extended to include a fifth group, the Variegated Leaf Group. Marco Hoffman is taxonomist and editor in chief of Dendroflora, a joint publication of the RBHS (Royal Boskoop Horticultural Society) and the NDV (Dutch Dendrological Society).

The five groups into which the cultivars have been classified and their characteristics are as follows:

Funnel Group
The leaves are usually evergreen.
The bract of the inflorescence usually opens on one side.
The flower is funnel-shaped and upright, horizontal or slightly arching. The diameter of the flower is of the same measurement as the length of the flower but usually more. The segments are not overlapping.

Trumpet Group
The leaves are either evergreen or deciduous.
The bract of the inflorescence opens either on one or two sides.
The flower is trumpet-shaped and upright to horizontal or facing slightly downwards. The diameter of the flower is the same as the length of the flower but usually less. The segments are usually overlapping.

Salver Group

The leaves are usually deciduous.
The bract of the inflorescence usually opens on one side. The flower is salver-shaped, horizontal or facing slightly downwards. The segments do not overlap each other or do so only at the base.

Tubular Group

The leaves are deciduous.
The bract of the inflorescence opens on one side. The flower is tubular and hanging. The segments overlap each other over the whole length.

Variegated Leaf Group

The leaves are deciduous or evergreen and variegated.

Agapanthus 'Septemberhemel', the blue colour is caused by anthocyanin

Each cultivar has a code that states to which group the plant belongs, if it is blue or white and if it is an evergreen or deciduous plant.

Anthocyanin

The blue colouring in *Agapanthus* is caused by anthocyanin. Anthocyanin is a flower colour pigment that is dissolved in the cytoplasm.

White-flowering *Agapanthus* can be divided into two groups: plants having green buds and pure white flowers, probably originating from *Agapanthus praecox*, and plants having purple buds and white flowers tinged purple. This group probably originates from *A. campanulatus* and *A. caulescens*. The pure white flowers of the first group contain no anthocyanin, the flowers of the second group do. The degree of anthocyanin in the plant is dependent on the sunlight. Plants growing in full sunlight have a higher percentage of anthocyanin than those plants which are growing in the shade. A plant that contains anthocyanin has a slightly purple-coloured leaf base. This does not imply that anthocyanin is present in the plant. It is possible for a plant to have a purple leaf base but pure white flowers, and then it contains no anthocyanin.

Garden

Evergreen *Agapanthus* seen in the
French Agapanthe garden

Choosing

The most important choice is between a deciduous and an evergreen plant. The choice is dependent on the possibilities available for overwintering. Whoever has no light and no frost-free spot, where the temperature does not exceed 8C, should not buy an evergreen plant, although it is possible for the plant to be kept at a firm specialised in housing plants during the winter months. A deciduous plant is easier to maintain during the winter because this plant requires no daylight during the winter; however, the overwintering temperature for this plant must also not exceed 8C.

If you already have an *Agapanthus* but do not know if it is deciduous or evergreen, you only have to look at the plant in October to see if the foliage is dying off. If this is the case then it is deciduous. Evergreen plants lose some of their leaves in autumn but not all. Next, it is important to know whether you want to put the plant in a tub or in the border. Both deciduous and evergreen plants can be grown in tubs, but only deciduous plants are suitable for the border.

After the place and the overwintering situation has been decided, then the rest is a question of taste. Some people like blue, others white. The colour blue varies from light greyish-blue to very dark blue, with many varieties in between. White is not just white, for there are white flowers with dark bracts and flower stalks that are even tinged with purple. There are also pure white flowers with yellowish-green bracts and green pedicels, which give an impression of pure white.

Such details as the height of the peduncle also play a role; this height varies from miniature plants such as 'Lilliput', whose peduncles can be 20 to 60 cm long, to huge plants like 'Blue Giant', whose peduncles can reach a height of 150 cm. The size of the umbels too varies enormously; the inflorescence of 'Bressingham Blue' has a diameter of 12 cm whereas that of 'Ellamae' has a diameter of 22 cm. The number of flowers

Deciduous *Agapanthus* in the
garden of Coates Manor, England

Agapanthus 'Bressingham
Blue' in the border

forming the umbel varies greatly, from 10 to more than 100 flowers. The number is more or less related to the size of the umbel. The shape of the umbel varies from flat to round. Then there are the various flower shapes, funnel, trumpet, salver and tubular, that either appeal to the garden lover or not. All these various qualities together give a total impression of the plant that remains in one's mind's eye or not.

Some people are bowled over by the largest and tallest plants, others choose the lower plants with smaller umbels (flower heads) and still others will choose an *Agapanthus* that has variegated foliage. It is always a question of taste; there is a suitable *Agapanthus* for everyone, so it is such a pity that some plants are just sold without names, for then you do not know which cultivar it is and how it has to be treated. Moreover, nine times out of ten it will be a plant of inferior quality.

Purchasing

One cannot be careful enough when purchasing an *Agapanthus*. If you see large clumps of *Agapanthus* at a flower sale, do not buy them. They are usually plants from flower growers. Flowers have been produced on these plants for years

and have only been discarded because their flowers have become inferior. These plants have never got a name; usually there will be only a tag with "love flower" or something similar written on it. The naïve purchaser, who thinks that only two varieties exist, the blue and the white, will be very tempted to pick up such a cash-desk bargain and that is a pity. Such a plant is certainly not representative of the genus and will, in spite of good care, flower poorly or not at all.

Never buy an *Agapanthus* in a plastic bag, for they have been treated as flower bulbs. A few roots between some peat moss will be provided with an attractive label with the name *Agapanthus* white or *Agapanthus* blue, and that is that. You will then just have to wait and see what it develops into. Bags are also sold bearing the name miniature *Agapanthus* and a blue flower head. This plant has nothing whatever to do with *Agapanthus* and is sailing under a false flag. If you have your specs on you will, upon closer inspection, be able to read in small letters *Brodiaea*. This is a perfectly good bulb but has nothing in common with an *Agapanthus*.

Never buy an *Agapanthus* in a pot that only bears the name *Agapanthus* blue or *Agapanthus* white because you will still

The Coen Jansen Perennials Nursery at Dalfsen

not know what you have got. It can be a beautiful plant, but it can also be a plant that hardly flowers and when it does they are not what you have been expecting. Never buy a plant bearing the name *Agapanthus africanus*, because this name is wrong. This species grows in South Africa, in the Western Cape, and is not grown anywhere in Europe. Do not buy an *A. umbellatus*, this name means nothing at all; it was given to *A. africanus* in 1789, discarded in 1824 and replaced by *A. africanus*. Whoever still uses the name *A. umbellatus* is a few centuries behind the times.

Certainly never buy Headbourne Hybrids, and do not believe it when they bear the words "winter hardy". Nowadays this name is a collective name for all sown *Agapanthus* and everything ripe and green is sold under this name. So do not be tempted. Now that interest in *Agapanthus* is growing it is to be hoped that garden centres will offer good cultivars of these plants for sale. Some already do, but even these may still bear a label with only white or blue on it because no others are available. It is quite a nice idea to put them to the test. If a group of plants are on offer under the same cultivar name, inspect the base of the leaves. If one plant has green at the base and another has purple, then they are plants which have been raised from seed and should not bear the name of a cultivar. If all the plants are exactly the same size, they can be from seed but

they can also be plants that have been micropropagated. Plants grown from micropropagation are true to the species and have the qualities of their parent plants; but because *Agapanthus* nomenclature is such a gigantic tangle, it sometimes occurs that the parent plant was not given the correct name, and therefore the offspring bear the wrong name too. A plant that has been multiplied by micropropagation has one point of growth, called the nose, often with many small noses growing next to it; a plant that has been vegetatively propagated by splitting is distinguished by several noses of the same size in one container.

It would seem that the garden lover should refrain from buying any *Agapanthus*, but that is not the general idea. Forewarned is forearmed, and it would be a pity if, after a couple of bad experiences, *Agapanthus* was given the blame and considered an impossible plant.

So it is most important to go in search of a reliable and experienced nurseryman who sells plants bearing a name. Then you can choose a plant that you find attractive and would like to have either in your garden or in a container.

Misunderstandings

A few misunderstandings persist in cropping up. It is said that a plant with broad leaves is evergreen and a plant with narrow leaves is deciduous. This is not true: there are evergreens with narrow leaves and deciduous plants with broad leaves. It is also said that evergreens are not winter hardy but deciduous plants are, and narrow-leaved plants are more winter hardy than broad-leaved specimens. Again, neither statement is true. Not one *Agapanthus* is winter hardy, however much growers proclaim otherwise. It is true that evergreens are definitely not winter hardy whereas deciduous plants can usually survive the winter provided they are well protected.

It has long been accepted that we must consider the original habitat of a plant in order to determine under which circumstances it will thrive, and *Agapanthus* is no exception. It appears that the evergreens grow in regions where it rains all winter and sometimes the whole year. This means that they continue to grow throughout the year. Therefore the ever-

Agapanthus in the Manoir de Saussey garden in France

Agapanthus in pots in the Agapanthe garden, France

greens must be kept in a lighted space during the winter and occasionally watered. Deciduous *Agapanthus* may be kept dry and in the dark during the winter because in the wild they occur in regions where it is dry in winter and only rains in summer.

Another misunderstanding is that the plants must only be repotted when absolutely necessary and given little nourishment in order for them to flourish. This is nonsense; like other plants, *Agapanthus* needs space and good soil in order to flower well.

Soil

Plants always do better planted out in the garden, where there is sufficient space for the roots and the nutrient situation is generally better than in the restricted space of a container. The plants, whether evergreen or deciduous, can grow in the border and be treated similarly to bulbs because they are less dependent on the type of soil than plants with "normal" roots. Generally speaking all types of soil are suitable, provided the water can drain away quickly enough; like so many other plants, *Agapanthus* does not like wet feet. Compost can be added to sandy soil so that it retains moisture better. In order to give clay better drainage, compost can be mixed with the soil. Add grit, especially in peat and clay soil The acid level is unimportant.

Potted plants require good, fertile soil; mixes are readily available in shops. Do not put the plant in ordinary compost; rather, mix two parts compost with one part sharp or river sand; some clay can also be added. The container should be sufficiently strong or stabilised in one way or another: *Agapanthus* can become very large and heavy, and the wind can blow a plant over. If the plant is in a large plastic pot, put this in a heavy stone or metal container, taking care that drainage is possible; excess water must be able to drain away. A container plant has to be repotted every three or four years and often divided. It is not necessary to repot every year. Plants that are not repotted can suffice with a fresh layer of topsoil. Do not believe it when it is said that an *Agapanthus* that is potbound will flower well. This is certainly not true. Repot a plant immediately after flowering when the soil is still warm. The plant will then form new roots before the winter.

Although the plant dislikes wet feet, it needs a large amount of water in the growing and flowering season. A plant in a container should be placed on a saucer, which is kept replenished with water. Owners of *Agapanthus* plants in containers cannot go on holiday unless they come to some arrangement with the neighbours or install a sprinkler system.

Agapanthus in pots,
Lacor's collection at
Kruiningen

Sun

The most frequently asked question, "Why isn't my *Agapanthus* flowering?", can be answered by considering where it is planted. In South Africa the plants grow in the sun, in the scorching sun, and they thrive. Even more important, they need sunlight to form buds for the following year. So if *Agapanthus* does not flower it has had insufficient sunlight the previous year or too little good fertiliser – this is possible – or it has been kept too warm during the winter. Both the plant in the border and the plant in a pot need sunlight not only for the formation of flower buds but also to keep the peduncle straight. These peduncles always incline towards the light, and if the plant is in too much shade they go in search of the sun and forget they are attached to something. The only plant that does not do this is *Agapanthus inapertus*, but this is an exception anyway with its nodding flowers.

People often are advised to put pots with plants that are not yet in flower or that have finished flowering away out of sight. This is fine as long as "out of sight" does not imply out of the sunlight, otherwise they will certainly not flower the following summer. In a spot that is too sunny and hot, they need a little shade, even though bent peduncles will be the result.

Nourishment

Good nourishment is good flowering. But what is good nourishment? Much can be learned from flower growers. They grow deciduous *Agapanthus* outside in the garden and give them a thick, protective layer of straw in winter. After removing the winter layer – when there is no further danger of frost – the plants are given some dried cow manure. The NPK (nitrogen, phosphorus and potassium) balance for this compost is 10-4-8. The nitrogen content is the highest because it provides good growth. Fertilisation with artificial fertiliser follows in which the NPK level is 7-14-28; the potassium content is now highest as this ensures good flowering. Seven kilos of this fertiliser is used per 100 sq. metres. At the end of the summer this application is repeated, but with half the amount of fertiliser, 3.5 kilos per 100 sq. metres.

From this we learn that both plants in the border and in pots should be given a handful of dried cow manure in spring and, once in flower, an application of fertiliser with an NPK level of 7-14-28. It is probably easier to dissolve the fertiliser in water before feeding it to the plant. It is preferable to pour the dissolved fertiliser onto the saucer rather than onto the topsoil. The high percentage of potassium in the fertiliser encourages the plant to form new flower buds. Such a fertiliser can be found in the vegetable and flower corner of the garden centre (fertilisers for tomatoes and strawberries have a high potassium content). No fertiliser should be given to the plant after September because it is then entering a rest period.

Winter

However much we would want it otherwise, *Agapanthus* is not winter hardy. Evergreen species and cultivars may not be kept in the garden, and all plants in containers must be taken indoors when it is freezing. However, the temperature does not say everything. A wet winter can cause more damage than a cold winter. Wet soil can create more havoc than a few days of frost. Ignace van Doorslaer, the Belgian breeder and collector of *Agapanthus*, keeps evergreen plants over in an unheated polytunnel, under a thick layer of straw, of course. These plants require no water. Evergreen plants in containers need light watering once every six weeks.

Fertilising cut flowers

Depending on the weather, deciduous plants in the garden should be covered at the end of autumn or the beginning of winter. This must not be done if the weather is still warm and certainly not earlier than October, and all leaves that have not yet fallen off should be removed, otherwise the plant will rot. Then cover the plant with a layer of straw. Put a layer of transparent plastic (with or without holes) over the straw and then add a second layer of straw. To prevent the straw's blowing away, place a piece of horticultural fleece over the straw and either dig it in at the sides or anchor it down with stones. Do not put the plastic in direct contact with the plant because this can cause rotting. At the end of the winter, when no more severe frosts are expected, the second layer of straw and the plastic under it may be removed. Leave the lower layer of straw in place for the time being. After having given the plants their spring feed, cut flower

growers cover this layer of straw with fleece and leave it on until the end of May, when there is no more danger of night frosts. But in the garden the winter cover may be removed earlier, in March. If there should be a night frost the plant can be temporarily covered with fleece. Instead of straw, the plant can also be covered with leaves and fir tree branches or with branches from the Christmas tree.

Agapanthus requires a cold period in order to flower well. This is something to be taken into consideration when keeping plants in containers during the winter. We can do our best to protect the plants from frost, but if they are kept too warm they will not flower. It is therefore advisable to keep the plants outside as long as possible and only bring them inside when it starts freezing. If the weather clears up after a short period of frost, then it would be better to put the

Seedlings

Seed capsules of *Agapanthus* 'Black Beauty'

plants outside again until the following period of frost. The maximum temperature for *Agapanthus* is 8C. If it is warmer then especially the deciduous plants will suffer, flowering poorly or not at all.

Take care that the temperature for evergreen plants does not drop beneath freezing. Deciduous plants can withstand a few degrees of frost. If the winter temperature for evergreens is too high, they will flower earlier and the peduncles will not be as sturdy. An evergreen plant needs a little water occasionally, a deciduous plant hardly any at all. An evergreen also needs light and may not be put into a dark garage. A deciduous plant does not require daylight.

If it is not freezing, put the plants outside at the end of April, preferably on a cloudy or, even better, on a rainy day. Pay attention to the weather forecast because as soon as frost is expected they have either to be taken indoors or given very good protection. They can only be left outside with confidence after mid May, when there can be no chance of a night frost. An unexpected hail shower in spring can strongly damage the foliage but will have no influence on the flowers.

Propagating

Sowing, dividing and lately also micropropagation are the various ways in which *Agapanthus* can be propagated.

Sowing

Agapanthus is easy to sow, and this is one reason there is such a mix-up in names within this genus. Cultivars should always be propagated vegetatively by division because this is the only means of knowing that the offspring will be identical to their parents. The fact that they can be excellently sown also has its advantages. Breeders can produce new plants by purposely crossbreeding, resulting in plants with even better qualities than the parent plants.

Plants in the garden should be able to set seed. This has no detrimental effect on the plant. The seed heads on a number of cultivars are exceptionally decorative and remain on the plant for quite some time. The triangular fruits are usually green, sometimes tinted purple and sometimes completely purple or so dark that they appear to be almost black. The fruits burst open on three sides. If you wish to harvest the seeds you have to be on time, otherwise they will fall on the ground. It is advisable to pick the seed heads when they are brown but not yet open. They can then continue to ripen indoors. Just like other seeds, *Agapanthus* seed must be stored in a dry and cool place and can be sown at the beginning of spring. In a warm climate it is advisable to sow *Agapanthus* as soon as it is ripe. Sow in special sowing compost or compost mixed with grit. The seed should not be covered. Cover the seed tray or the pots with plastic so that the ground does not dry out. Remove the plastic when the seeds have started to germinate, after three or four weeks. If the seed has been sown far enough apart, then the seedlings will not need to be transplanted the first year. It will take at least three years before the plants flower.

Division

A plant that has been produced by division will have the same qualities as the parent plant. This is, therefore, the best way to propagate cultivars. However, most garden lovers will not divide plants to obtain more plants but because the plant has outgrown its pot or has become unmanageable in the border. An *Agapanthus* must be divided with utmost care. There are plants that can be split up into several pieces with a spade but an *Agapanthus* has to be handled very carefully, otherwise too many wounds will occur, which heal with difficulty, or the plant can become infected with a fungus.

First of all, rinse the clump of roots clean with water, so that you can see what you are doing. Then divide the clump into several parts with a sharp knife and put them straight into pots or into the garden. The best time to divide an *Agapanthus* is just after flowering, when the plants are still in their growing season and will continue to grow after division. The plant then recovers more quickly than it would in winter or spring. Thick old roots can be divided into separate pieces. If each piece has a few roots and buds it will sprout and form new plants.

Micropropagation

Micropropagation is another method of vegetative propagation used for *Agapanthus*. There are several methods and techniques but, in general, it entails putting a minute growing point of a plant onto a propagation tray, and this will develop into a very small plant. This minute plant is grown in completely sterile surroundings, and after six to eight weeks it will again be divided. The speed at which the plant is propagated is closely connected to the propagation factor,

and this is dependent on the type of plant. A plant that has a propagation factor of 3 can produce more than 60,000 plants in one year. But there are limits to micropropagation, and it is impossible to continue propagating with cell tissue from the same plants indefinitely. Micropropagation is often compared to babies in an incubator: they need great care at first, afterwards they thrive but later it appears that there is something wrong with some of the babies. Cut flower growers sometimes find that plants obtained by micropropagation produce poorer flowers. Moreover, it seems that 3 to 5% of the plants are not true to the parent plants, and that was the desired goal, originally.

Pests and diseases

Agapanthus is an exceptionally strong plant that is seldom troubled by pests and diseases. The problems that garden lovers meet with are those concerned with flowering, not those related to annoying pests and diseases. All those mentioned here "can" occur but usually *Agapanthus* is unaffected by them. However, plants that have been in culture for some time are prone to virus infections. New cultivars are virus-free, and those obtained by micropropagation are also virus-free. Plants that have been infected by a virus will not immediately die but after a number of years they will flower less profusely. You can see whether a plant has been infected by a virus by looking at the leaves, which will have lighter coloured stripes on them.

Warm and damp weather can often lead to botrytis, a fungal infection that will cause red stripes on the leaves and the stems; it has little influence on the plant so nothing need be done about it. A fungus that affects only *Agapanthus* is *Macrophomina agapanthi*; the foliage shows brown spots that start at the base and spread over the whole leaf. The fungus *Phytophthora* tends to dry up the leaves from the base and the roots can rot; it can also affect the flowers.

During warm summers red spider mites and thrips can be a nuisance, as can woolly aphids, cottony maple scale, green fly, mealy bugs, scale insects and aphids, occasionally. In spring, the young foliage can be damaged by slugs and snails, but this is generally not serious and the plant quickly recovers.

Fasciations

Occasionally *Agapanthus* is affected by certain deformities called fasciations. These are abnormalities or rarities that are sometimes peculiar to one cultivar and sometimes not. For instance, the peduncle is exserted through the inflorescence (what is known as pagoda growth); this can occur with evergreen cultivars that have just been repotted. Then the flowers often have more than the usual six tepals, as can occur in a few double flowering cultivars. A feature of such double flowers is that they hardly ever open fully.

The inflorescence of *Agapanthus* is composed of groups or internodes, which do not all open simultaneously. Occasionally, elongated internodes appear so that the flowers on the inflorescence are not spread evenly.

There are also cultivars that suddenly produce double flowers that do open. This is a temporary deviation, and it appears that the stamens have become tepals. Sometimes two penduncles are joined together like Siamese twins and produce two inflorescences as if they were one. This is very rare.

Still another strange fasciation is when a cluster of flowers appears on the peduncle just under the inflorescence or even lower. This fasciation occurs on other plants, such as the poppy, and some cultivars have even been developed with this deviation. A poppy with a collar of small seed boxes under the large seed head bears the cultivar name 'Hen and Chickens'. When this fasciation appears on an *Agapanthus* plant it is also called "Hen and Chickens".

Situation

There is always a space to be found for *Agapanthus* in pots. Put them in a sheltered spot in the sun and take care that they are not in the way. They are sturdy plants, and it would be a great pity if these leaves, which have been nurtured with care, snapped off because someone bumped into them. A terrace is an ideal place. An *Agapanthus* should be placed in a conspicuous spot. It is not a plant to be pushed into any odd corner. They attract a great deal of attention when they are in flower and, therefore, they cannot be combined with just any old plant. A guaranteed success is *Agapanthus* with clipped box balls. This combination is also most suitable for

Fasciations

plants in the garden. The box balls, with their small leaves, form a strong contrast to the large *Agapanthus* leaves and provide a restful green background for the flowers. Such a combination makes the *Agapanthus* even more striking than it already is. *Agapanthus* plants are found all over Madeira, where a row of variegated plants is often seen on a flight of stairs, one container on each step.

Combinations

The plant can, of course, be combined with other border plants in the garden. Whoever likes strong contrasts should try blue *Agapanthus* with orange *Crocosmia* 'Lucifer' or with yellow *Heliopsis helianthoides* var. *scabra* 'Spitzentänzerin'. A delightful combination is dark blue *Agapanthus* with greenish-yellow *Euphorbia schillingii*. Blue *Agapanthus* also looks lovely with yellow *Helenium*, red *Knautia* and the pinkish-red umbels of *Sedum spectabile*. Blue *Agapanthus* with yellow *Oenothera* is a striking combination, for the floppy evening primrose forms a beautiful contrast beside the sturdy, elegant *Agapanthus* flower heads. The same colour contrast is achieved when planting blue *Agapanthus* together with yellow *Achillea,* but in this combination the *Agapanthus* flowers appear looser when compared to the stiff, compact umbels of the *Achillea.*

A tone-on-tone combination is achieved with dark blue *Agapanthus* and *Perovskia* 'Blue Spire'. In England one sees many *Agapanthus* plants combined with *Penstemon* and this is very beautiful but the *Penstemon* must be treated as an annual because it does not survive the winter easily. A wonderful combination is blue *Agapanthus* with one of the lovely red cultivars of *Persicaria amplexicaule,* with some touch-me-not flowers, *Impatiens glandulifera,* scattered amongst them. In Beth Chatto's famous gravel garden, the yellow *Clematis tibetana* subsp. *vernayi* creeps around the foot of a blue *Agapanthus.* The latter also looks wonderful when combined with grey foliage perennials or bushes, such as *Lavandula, Eucalyptus, Artemisia stelleriana, Stachys byzantina* and *Convolvulus cneorum.*

White *Agapanthus* fits in splendidly in a white garden when combined with the white flowering plumes of *Artemisia lactiflora* or with the white willow-herb *Chamerion angustifolium* 'Album'. Both white and blue *Agapanthus* combine well with grasses, although the leaves of the grasses are so much finer than the *Agapanthus* leaves that the latter then appear very coarse. *Molinia caerulea* subsp. *arundinacea* 'Transparant', a very delicate, overhanging grass, creates a cloud around the stiff peduncles of *Agapanthus,* just like *Panicum virgatum* 'Rehbraun'. An *Agapanthus,* blue or white, looks wonderful beside a rosemary bush, and the advantage is that both require shelter from the cold and wet of winter.

The holder of the English NCCPG *Agapanthus,* Dick Fulcher, sells plants that can be used in combination with *Agapanthus* at his nursery, Pine Cottage Plants. He considers the following to be good neighbours: the brick-red-with-purple *Agastache* 'Firebird', the pink *Argyranthemum* 'Gills Pink' and the pale yellow *Argyranthemum* 'Jamaica Primrose'. Several cannas are useful such as the huge *Canna* x*ehemanii,* which has dark pink flowers, the extremely large

leaved *C.* 'Musifolia', *C.* 'Rosemond Coles', with yellow-margined orange flowers, and *C.* ' Striata' with yellow-striped leaves and orange flowers. *Cautleya spicata* 'Robusta', with leaves that resemble the foliage of *Hedychium* and orange yellow flowers, looks exotic enough to rival *Agapanthus.*

Eucomis pole-evansii, with green leaves, and *E.* 'Zeal Bronze', with bronze-coloured leaves, can also rival *Agapanthus.* Like *Canna, Diascia* and *Argyranthemum,* they are not winter hardy and need care. The white *Galtonia can-*

Agapanthus and *Crocosmia*

Agapanthus 'Meibont' with *Sedum*

Agapanthus with *Knautia,* Buscot Park, England

Agapanthus 'Marianne' with evening primrose, Leiden

dicans and pale green *G. viridiflora* are also not hardy but mix well with *Agapanthus* because they also hail from South Africa, just as *Eucomis* and *Watsonia* do. *Watsonia borbonica* subsp. *ardernei* 'Arderne's White', with white flowers, *W. fulgens*, with bright red flowers, *W. pillansii*, with orange flowers, and *W.* Tresco hybrids, with flowers that vary in colour from pink to orange, also originate from South Africa and are not hardy either.

Hedychium coccineum 'Tara', *H. densiflorum* 'Assam Orange' and *H. gardnerianum*, are all most spectacular plants with their brick red, deep orange and cream with yellow flowers, and look delightful with *Agapanthus* but, again, are not hardy. *Nemesia denticulata* (syn. *N.* 'Confetti') can continue to flower into the autumn and form a pink cloud from which the peduncles of white and blue *Agapanthus* arise. Pale pink cultivars of *Phlox paniculata* create a sweet combination with pale blue *Agapanthus* and the playful, but not hardy, *Salvia microphylla* 'Pink Blush' and *S. involucrata* 'Bethellii' make *Agapanthus* look less strict and rigid.

Agapanthus with *Penstemon*

Agapanthus with giant balsam

The sweet-smelling pale purple *Verbena* 'La France' and the pale pink fading to silver white *V.* 'Silver Anne' are also excellent combined with *Agapanthus*. Plants that are not hardy can also be treated like tub plants and then combined with tubs of *Agapanthus*. Keep the plants apart, do not plant them together in one container. It appears that *Agapanthus*, which is usually considered a solitary plant and beautiful enough in its own right, is very attractive when combined

Agapanthus with *Clematis tibetana* subsp. *vernayi*, Beth Chatto

Agapanthus 'Bressingham Blue' with *Kniphofia*

Agapanthus with pale pink *Phlox*, at Iford Manor, England

Agapanthus 'Septemberhemel' w Helenium and Helianthus salicifo

Agapanthus in a public
garden in Portugal

Agapanthus praecox
'Albiflorus' on Madeira

with other late-flowering border and container plants. Perhaps the idea takes a little getting used to but that is also what we had to do with the alliums, and these bulbs are now extremely popular.

Naturalizing

Agapanthus will certainly not naturalize in countries with a temperate climate, but in countries where it hardly ever freezes they feel very much at home. Both white and blue *Agapanthus* thrive extremely well along the west coast of the North Island of New Zealand. They are to be found in the dunes and appear to be completely immune to the salty wind that blows from the Tasman Sea. *Agapanthus* flourishes on the island of Madeira as if it were growing in its natural habitat. California provides the ideal climate for *Agapanthus*, and garden lovers have an enormous choice of plants and need never worry about frost.

However, *Agapanthus* can thrive so well that the plants sometimes pose a threat to the indigenous flora. In New Zealand *Agapanthus* is to be uprooted from those places where it grows in the wild. It could be that in the future they will be banned from gardens or perhaps only sterile plants that do not produce seed will be permitted. The same method could be applied to other warm areas where *Agapanthus* is flourishing so well that the local flora is suffering.

Cut Flowers

Bunches of *Agapanthus* at
a market in Portugal

Place of origin

Agapanthus is an excellent cut flower, but it would never
enter a garden lover's head to pick the flowers of this stately
plant in his own garden. We prefer to leave the growing of
cut flowers to professional cut flower growers.

More and more *Agapanthus* flowers are appearing in florists'
shops, and many of them are grown in The Netherlands.
The quality of the *Agapanthus* cultivars that are grown
abroad is considerably inferior to that of cultivars from The
Netherlands. Moreover, the colours are far inferior. The
number of *Agapanthus* peduncles delivered to the flower
auctions has grown steadily from 3.8 million in 1995 to 7.5
million in 2002.

Agapanthus is also grown as a cut flower in South Africa and
exported to the United States and Europe. The cut flowers
grown in South America are exported to the United States.
Agapanthus flowers that are grown in Japan from mid summer until mid winter are sold on the home market, and during the winter and in spring they are imported from other
countries. In New Zealand they are grown on a small scale,
mainly for the home market. Although *Agapanthus* is to be
found almost year-round, the cut flowers are usually sold in
the summer months. *Agapanthus* is grown for its cut flowers
in the western part of Australia, and they are available for
sale from the beginning of September.

Best choice and care

There is of course a reason why *Agapanthus* is becoming
more popular as a cut flower. It is excellent in flower
arrangements and remains fresh for a long time in a vase.
Cut flower growers choose the best cultivars, use the appropriate cultivation methods and give their customers advice as
to how they should treat the flowers.

The choice of cultivars is important with regard to the loss
of buds, which appears to be related to the influence of

Picking cut flowers

A field of *Agapanthus* at Kees Duivenvoorde's nursery

Agapanthus africanus. Cultivars that have *A. africanus* in their background should really not be used for the cut flower industry, nor for breeding new cultivars. It is known that 'Wolga' and 'Amsterdam' are more inclined to lose their buds, but it is not always a question of cultivar. Growing conditions are also important: the plants will lose more buds if it is dry during the growing period. Plants grown in greenhouses will show less bud loss because the atmosphere is damp. The same applies to plants grown outside during a period of rain.

The flowers are often protected by a net during transport so that they will not be damaged. Naturally, this net will have to be removed before the stalk is cut slantwise with a sharp knife. The flowers will remain fresh for a longer period if cut flower food is added to the water. Do not put too much water in the vase, but keep it refilled. If the flowers are to be used in oasis, which is a good option, then the oasis must first be immersed in water to which cut flower food has been added. Please note that *Agapanthus* flowers are sensitive to the influence of ethylene gas, which is given off by ripening fruit. So take care not to stand them near a bowl of fruit.

A longer season

Several years ago the research station PPO Horst (Praktijk Onderzoek Plant & Omgeving = practical research into plants and their surroundings) carried out trials in order to force late flowering of *Agapanthus*. This is interesting for growers, not only for the price but for the staggering of the labour force. It appears that it is possible to delay flowering for two months. The plants are dug up one to four weeks

after flowering and planted in boxes. These boxes are kept under certain well-controlled conditions with an exceptionally low oxygen content (a special ULO cell). Ordinary cold storage is also implemented; although this method produces fewer peduncles, it can be of interest to the growers. The plants are taken outside in week 23. This could be done at a later stage, but should there be an early frost the crop could be lost, unless a tunnel is placed over the plants. So it is possible to produce *Agapanthus* plants that flower two months later by keeping them under the correct storage conditions in boxes during the winter and taking them outside in the summer.

Fields full of flowers

In the province of North Holland cut flowers are grown out of doors. The "geestgronden" (the sheltered area of sandy soil between the dunes and the polder in The Netherlands) has long been famous for its excellent soil for bulbs. *Agapanthus* requires aerated soil. The flowers are grown from deciduous cultivars and are given a thick cover of straw in winter. Every three or four years the plants are dug up out of the ground, divided and replanted. Young plants produce more flowers per square meter, and it is a magnificent sight to see a whole field of flowering *Agapanthus*.

The plants are cut down to ground level with a lawn mower before the winter sets in so that the leaves will not rot under the winter cover. Afterwards, a layer of old straw, which no longer contains weed seeds, is put over the plants, followed by a layer of transparent plastic and, on top of this, a final layer of fresh straw is added. This amounts to 300 kilos of

The plants are mown down by a lawn mower before the winter

The protective fleece is removed when there is no longer a threat of frost

Kees Duivenvoorde, breeder

straw per 100 square metres. The first layer of straw can be thinner than the second. In spring the top layer of straw and the plastic are removed. The lower layer of straw remains over the plants and provides good ground cover against weeds and silting up of the soil. Now is the time to apply dried cow manure, preferably just before a shower, otherwise the soil must be watered afterwards. Then a horticultural fleece is put over the plants and anchored down at the sides. This is left until the end of May to be certain that the very last night frost cannot cause any damage. When the fleece is removed the plants will be about 10 cm tall. The plants are then given a topping of artificial fertiliser with an NPK ratio of 7-14-28. If it has been a wet winter and many of the nutrients have been washed away, then a second application of fertiliser will be necessary. The plants should not be given too much nitrogen, otherwise the foliage will grow at the cost of the flowers. Peduncles are cut as soon as a few flowers have opened.

Suitable cultivars

The Dutch breeder Kees Duivenvoorde became involved with *Agapanthus* thirty years ago. He aspired to grow a dark cultivar with large flowers. The first *Agapanthus* to attract his attention was 'Intermedius'. He bought some plants, divided and planted them according to the instructions, but they did not flower. The following year only a few flowers blossomed. The dark blue colour was delightful but there were too few flowers and, therefore, it was not suitable for cut flower cultivation. So he then began to deliberately crossbreed and select new plants. Cultivars from the Dutch breeder Schoehuys, which were new at the time, produced far more flowers, so together with *A*. 'Intermedius' they formed the basis for the breeding.

"Breeding entails throwing away", according to Duivenvoorde. "Your first seedlings will be equally beautiful, but the new plants have to be first class and, moreover, must not resemble the cultivars that are already in existence". Counting from the moment of crossbreeding it takes about ten years before a new cultivar can be registered. After the crossbreeding, seed will be produced that has to be sown in January. In June the seedlings can be taken outside. They remain in the ground outside for two years (with a winter

"Breeding is a matter of throwing away"   *Agapanthus* 'Volendam', Huis Verwolde   Catharina Duivenvoorde with *Agapanthus* 'Catharina'

cover, of course). If they show difficulty in surviving then they must be relegated to the compost heap. They must be able to survive the winter under cover and prove this at an early age. The plants that do survive will start flowering after three years. A few beautiful plants are selected and the rest thrown away.

From 'Dr Brouwer' to 'Madurodam'

The first Kees Duivenvoorde cultivar to come onto the market, 'Dr Brouwer', was registered in 1987 and is still grown by cut flower producers. The plant flowers early; this flowering time is one of the characteristics that Duivenvoorde wished to exploit in the breeding of plants. When he first started this work the flowering time of an *Agapanthus* was about three weeks, whilst the early-flowering cultivars are now picked in June and the late ones in September. He has now selected 37 cultivars, which vary in flowering time from early to late in the season, in colours from white to dark blue, and with peduncles that vary in height from 30 to 125 cm. Many cultivars are used for the cut flower industry including not only the popular 'Dr Brouwer' but also 'Catharina', 'Columba', 'Edinburgh', 'Elisabeth', 'Johanna', 'Marianne', 'Prinses Marilène', 'Rotterdam' and 'Volendam'.

The interest in *Agapanthus* plants for the garden has grown during the past few years, and Duivenvoorde is now busy breeding beautiful new plants. This is not to imply that plants developed for the cut flower industry are not suitable

as garden and container plants. For example, a low-growing *Agapanthus* like the latest 'Madurodam' is a wonderful garden and pot plant but is unsuitable as a cut flower because the stalks are not long enough.

Duivenvoorde has not yet finished his work with *Agapanthus* and still has many surprises in store. In the course of the past few years he has built up an *Agapanthus* collection of more than 200 cultivars. The favourite is one of his most recent cultivars, *A.* 'Copenhagen'.

Thanks to people like Duivenvoorde, there are many good cultivars on the market that can be easily grown out of doors, produce a good crop and, moreover, are well suited to a vase. Florists and customers are happy with them, and so are garden lovers, who do not grow their plants in order to pick the flowers, but even so appreciate the beautiful colour, shape, length of the peduncle and profuse flowering of the cut flower cultivars.

Bouquets

Queen Beatrix was presented with a wonderful bouquet of *Agapanthus* combined with yellow roses at her birthday celebration in 2003. *Agapanthus* is increasingly used in bouquets and modern flower arrangements. The large ball of *Agapanthus* that graced the lawn of the Huis Verwolde estate during the first Dutch *Agapanthus* Days in 2003 was spectacular. It was made up of 800 peduncles, most of which

A flower arrangement of *Agapanthus* 'Johanna', 'Prinses Marilène', 'Parijs' and 'Marianne' by Martin Wijnbergen at Huis Verwolde

were the cultivar 'Dr Brouwer'. Most of the traditional rooms in Huis Verwolde were decorated with floral arrangements, and each bore the name of the cultivars included. Martin Wijnbergen, the florist who was responsible for these arrangements, had used more than 1600 peduncles, which had been supplied by cut flower growers. These experts told him that they had not taken the trouble to produce the long, straight stalks for nothing and would have liked to have seen them in the arrangement. However, the wreath made up of *Agapanthus, Hedera, Pachysandra, Pieris* and green *Sedum* flowers was greatly appreciated. The flowers stalks had been cut very short, it is true, but they had been integrated into the wreath in a most ingenious way.

Always in bud

'Buddy Blue' is an *Agapanthus* whose flowers never open. This cultivar was raised by Cape Seed & Bulb in South Africa by Jim Holms. The inflorescence on a 70- to 90-cm-tall peduncle has a diameter of 15 cm and consists of 50 to 60 buds. Because the buds never open, 'Buddy Blue' remains attractive in a vase of water for 12 to 18 days.

A wreath of *Agapanthus* 'Duná' made by
Martin Wijnbergen at Huis Verwolde

Detail of a wreath

A flower arrangement of *Agapanthus* 'Pinocchio'
by Martin Wijnbergen at Huis Verwolde

A flower arrangement of *Agapanthus* 'Pinocchio'
by Martin Wijnbergen at Huis Verwolde

Plant Collections

Agapanthus specialists Dick Fulcher
(England), Wim Snoeijer (The Netherlands)
and Ignace van Doorslaer (Belgium)

We wish to thank you most gratefully for the

trust you have placed in us with regard to our

expertise by allowing us to take over your most

carefully assembled collection.

30 September 2002, a letter from the director of

the Geldersch Landscape Foundation to Wim

Snoeijer, concerning the takeover of the

Agapanthus collection.

The Netherlands

In 1995 Wim Snoeijer, a plant fanatic who was then
employed by the Department of Pharmacognosy at Leiden
University, published an extensive article on *Agapanthus* in
the magazine of the Oranjerievereniging (Dutch Orangery
Society). Although the genus *Clematis* is his speciality – he
has been breeding and collecting everything to do with these
plants for years – he was also interested in the whole group
of monocotyledons, including *Agapanthus*. In order to collect information for his article, he visited nurseries at home
and abroad. He immersed himself in libraries and archives,
searching for information, and landed in a maze of confusing
literature, contradictory information and obscure nomenclature. After publishing the article he returned to *Clematis*
until, in 1996, he bought the new *RHS Plant Finder*. The list
of *Agapanthus* plants began with a spelling error. He then
decided to lengthen his study of *Agapanthus* by a year and
once again went in search of growers and information.

When the KAVB (Royal General Bulb Growers Association) organised the first *Agapanthus* trial in August 1996, Snoeijer discussed several subjects concerning this plant with Johan van Scheepen. One of these was the idea of setting up a collection of purely Dutch cultivars. Van Scheepen was very enthusiastic. The nurseries Duivenvoorde and Maas & van Stein immediately offered some plants so that the collection could be started. Only Dutch cultivars were collected because there was already a collection of all cultivars in England, and Snoeijer did not want to duplicate this.

Snoeijer was in charge of a large experimental garden at Leiden University, and in September 1996 the first cultivars were planted. At the same time they came up with a plan to do some research into the colour of flowers; *Agapanthus* would fit in well with this plan because blue *Agapanthus* contains the colour pigment anthocyanin. Whilst Snoeijer was getting his collection together he also issued his first *Agapanthus* Newsletter. Eventually, seven newsletters were sent to interested people in The Netherlands, Belgium, Canada, England, France, Northern Ireland, Japan, the United States and South Africa. The collection grew steadily in the course of the years, as did the number of peduncles. All data on the cultivars was collected, a detailed description given (colour was given by means of a colour code), slides were made and herbarium material was collected and kept at the Rijksherbarium (National Herbarium) in Leiden. The

collection began with 19 cultivars and now, in 2004, consists of 68 cultivars. New cultivars that have been won by Dutch breeders are still being added to the collection, and some old Dutch cultivars are being rediscovered.

In 1995, following the English example, Dutch Plant Collections had been set up by the RBHS (Royal Boskoop Horticultural Society); the *Agapanthus* collection of Dutch cultivars was officially named an NPC (Netherlands Plant Collection) in 1998. When Snoeijer changed jobs and the experimental garden at Leiden University was closed, the collection came into the possession of Het Geldersch Landschap, which exhibits the National Plant Collection at Rosendael Castle in the province of Gelderland, The Netherlands. Snoeijer still gives advice and looks after any additions to it. Gerard Achterstraat is now in charge of the collection.

In 2003 Snoeijer organised the Dutch *Agapanthus* Days at Huis Verwolde in Laren (province of Gelderland). The whole collection was exhibited, and breeders, both local and international, were present. From the overwhelming interest shown, it appears that *Agapanthus* is extremely popular, both as a cut flower and as a container plant. At the same time it turned out that there were still many misunderstandings and many *Agapanthus* admirers were in search of information.

Dutch *Agapanthus* days at Huis Verwolde; the large ball, made up of about 100 stalks of 'Dr Brouwer', is by Martin Wijnbergen

Snoeijer has meanwhile had his English-language botanical reference book, *Agapanthus: A Revision of the Genus*, published by the American publishing firm Timber Press; in it, all the species and cultivars are most carefully described. Which *Agapanthus* would such a person, who knows so much about the plant, find the most beautiful? Snoeijer does not need long to ponder this question. He considers 'Marianne' the most beautiful, closely followed by 'Septemberhemel'.

The *Agapanthus* collection of breeder Kees Duivenvoorde consists of more than 200 cultivars, 37 of which he has bred himself. Further information about Duivenoorde and his collection can be found in the chapter on Cut Flowers.

Great Britain

More than 20 years ago, when Dick Fulcher was working as head gardener at Inverewe Garden in Scotland, he had already started collecting *Agapanthus*. This plant thrives there because Inverewe is on the west coast of Scotland, where it hardly ever freezes because of the influence of the warm Gulf Stream. After ten years he moved to Devon in the southwest of England and became a lecturer at Bicton College, where he also was in charge of the gardens. He really got smitten then and built up a wonderful collection of *Agapanthus.* He also began to breed his own cultivars, of which there are now more than 35.

Now he has his own nursery, and *Agapanthus* is still his great love. He took his official NCCPG collection, which by now consists of more than 200 species and cultivars, to Pine Cottage in Eggesford in Devon. He grows more than 40 cultivars for sale, but still considers that he has a small nursery. At the present moment he has a new cultivar, a very dark one, as yet unnamed; he cannot decide whether it should be 'Queen of the Night' or 'Starlight'. His most beautiful *Agapanthus*? Without hesitation he names 'Purple Cloud'.

A second *Agapanthus* collection is to be found at Bicton Park. This collection, in the gardens of Bicton College, consists of 90 species and cultivars.

Agapanthus collection,
Kees Duivenvoorde

The Belgian grower and breeder
Ignace van Doorslaer

Belgium

Ignace van Doorslaer has been involved with *Agapanthus* for more than 15 years. His first plant was killed off by frost during the winter, which is why he decided to concentrate on plants that were reasonably capable of surviving the winter. He collects, propagates, crossbreeds and selects plants, the result of which is a number of lovely cultivars. His collection consists of more than 185 deciduous and evergreen cultivars. Van Doorslaer, who at first specialised in *Hosta* and with this genus achieved world fame, hails from a family of nurserymen. They grew orchids but, as a result of the oil crisis in the 1970s, Ignace decided to grow perennials and in this way became interested in hostas. *Agapanthus* was a new challenge, and with this plant he also became a famous grower. 'Stéphanie', 'Stéphanie Charm' and 'Sylvine' are cultivars that he has bred himself. 'Stéphanie Charm' is his favourite because he considers it a pretty, profusely flowering plant that can easily survive the winter in a warm garden or with suitable winter cover. This is also the case with 'Sylvine', which is a late flowerer.

For years van Doorslaer, convinced that there was such a one in 1800, has been searching for a pink *Agapanthus*, and he has nearly got there. The first time he imported 'Purple Cloud' from New Zealand he found a plant that seemed to be pink. He started to grow this plant. The plant that he is shortly to launch has a colour halfway between light and dark mauve. This "pink" *Agapanthus* is to be called 'Pinky'. The most beautiful *Agapanthus*? 'Stéphanie Charm', he responds.

Species

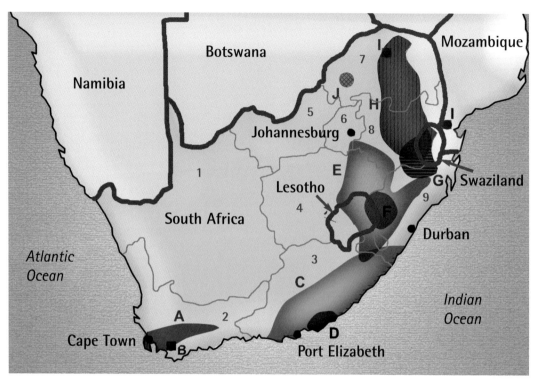

Main localities of the species

A   *A. africanus*
B. *A. africanus* subsp. *walshii*
C. *A. praecox*
D. *A. praecox* subsp. *minimus*
    (including *A. comptonii*)
E. *A. campanulatus*
F. *A. caulescens*
    (including *A. nutans*)
G. *A. caulescens*
H. *A. inapertus*
I. *A. inapertus* subsp. *intermedius*
    (including *A. dyeri*)
J. *A. coddii*

South African provinces

1   Northern Cape
2   Western Cape
3   Eastern Cape
4   Free State
5   North West
6   Gauteng
7   North
8   Mpumalanga
9   KwaZulu-Natal

Most of the species and subspecies are still available, some more easily than others. A PF (Plant Finder) or a PV (Dutch Plant Finder) indicates that a species or subspecies is available.

All *Agapanthus* species are indigenous to South Africa, from the Western Cape in the south to the mountainous regions south of the River Limpopo in the north. They are to be found from sea level to 2100 m high. An occasional species may be found at different heights.

The deciduous species grow in areas that have dry winters and rain in summer. The evergreens grow in regions where it either rains during the winter months or throughout the year. In their natural habitat the deciduous plants begin to grow as soon as the spring rains arrive. They thrive well because of the rain and produce their first flowers in mid summer. The evergreen species lose a few of their outer leaves, and these are replaced by new leaves. They have a long flowering period that commences at the end of spring or the beginning of summer. The main flowering season is in mid summer. The seeds are ripe in autumn, and these germinate after the first autumn rains. In regions where it rains in summer the seeds remain dormant until the spring rains.

According to the latest opinions, six different species and fourteen subspecies of the species have been distinguished. Of the six species, two are evergreen: *Agapanthus africanus* and *A. praecox*. The other four are deciduous: *A. campanulatus*, *A. caulescens*, *A. coddii* and *A. inapertus*.

Agapanthus africanus PF PV
The first description of *Agapanthus* in 1679 was of this species. The plant grows in the wild, mainly in the mountainous regions of the Western Cape, from sea level up to 1000 m, from the Cape Peninsula to Paarl and Stellenbosch and eastwards to Swellendam. This particularly variable species is extremely common in places where there is a great amount of rainfall, but it does not always flower. The height of the peduncle varies from 25 to 70 cm and the number of flowers per inflorescence from 12 to 30. The trumpet-shaped flower is dark violet blue, sometimes slightly paler, and occasionally white. The pollen is yellow. The flowering time in its country of origin is from December to April. It appears that this species flowers well after fires. Although this plant has been in cultivation since 1674, most of the plants that are nowadays on offer under this name are hybrids. Some plants are still being erroneously put on sale with this name, for this evergreen species is very difficult to propagate in cultivation. This is a protected species in South Africa.

Agapanthus africanus subsp. *africanus*
This subspecies is, just as the species itself, very variable and occurs in the Western Cape, around Bredasdorp, Caledon,

Paarl, Stellenbosch and Swellendam, from sea level up to 1000 m. The peduncle varies in length from 25 to 70 cm, and the inflorescence bears 12 to 30 flowers. The flower has a fleshy texture. The colour is dark violet blue, occasionally paler and only rarely white. The plants flower in their original habitat from December to April.

Agapanthus africanus subsp. *walshii* (was *A. walshii*)
This subspecies is found only in a small mountainous area in the southwestern region of the Western Cape, from Steenbras to Caledon, at a height of 450 to 730 m. The peduncle varies in length from 30 to 70 cm, and the number of flowers per inflorescence from 8 to 19. The flower is violet blue, only occasionally white, pendulous and tubular. The plant flowers in its place of origin in January and February. The plant was discovered in 1918, but when Lewis Palmer went in search of the plant in 1963 he was unsuccessful and found nothing. This subspecies is extremely difficult in cultivation. It requires well-drained soil. A mixture of equal parts acid, sandy soil and burnt soil is recommended, and a thick layer of gravel or grit should be put around the plant.

Agapanthus campanulatus PF PV
This deciduous species occurs from the centre of the provinces of KwaZulu-Natal, in Lesotho and in the Free State up into the northeastern region of the Eastern Cape, in grassy and rocky areas on moist soil. This species has been known in Great Britain since 1822. The peduncle varies in length from 30 to 100 cm, and the inflorescence bears 10 to 30 flowers. The salver-shaped flowers are pale to dark violet blue, only occasionally white. The flowers are not longer than 3.5 cm and the pollen is purple. Plants flower in their original habitat from December until the end of February.

Agapanthus campanulatus subsp. *campanulatus*
This subspecies occurs in many places in South Africa, e.g. KwaZulu-Natal and in the Eastern Cape, but does not grow at great heights. The flowers are bright violet blue; the tips of the petals do not open completely.

Agapanthus campanulatus subsp. *patens* PF PV
This subspecies is to be found in mountainous grassland, damp valleys, on damp slopes, basalt cliffs and other damp

Agapanthus campanulatus subsp. *patens*

places, at a height of 1800 to 2400 m, in the Free State, Lesotho, KwaZulu-Natal and Gauteng. The flower is bright blue and opens completely. Most of the plants that are grown under the name *A. campanulatus* are, in fact, this subspecies.

Agapanthus caulescens (syn. *A. nutans*) PF PV
This deciduous species is found in rocky areas, on grassy slopes and beside mountain streams and cliffs in KwaZulu-Natal, Swaziland and the southeastern region of Mpumalanga. These are large plants with a peduncle that varies in length from 60 to 180 cm and with an inflorescence that bears either a few or many flowers. The flower is dark violet blue with a paler base and a darker midrib. The segments of the flower are spread out and curl up. The flowers are more then 3.5 cm long and the pollen is purple. In its natural habitat this species flowers from November until

February. The Dutchman Sprenger received some seed of this species in 1890 from a friend, who had collected it in the former Transvaal. He sowed these seeds in his nursery in Naples; probably 'Blue Triumphator' was a selection from this species.

Agapanthus caulescens subsp. *angustifolius* PF
This very tall subspecies, with a peduncle of 100 cm, occurs in Swaziland, KwaZulu-Natal and Mpumalanga. The flower is very dark violet. The difference between this plant and the other subspecies is that the flower is smaller and the leaves are narrower and upright.

Agapanthus caulescens subsp. *caulescens* PF
This subspecies occurs in Swaziland alongside shaded river banks. The peduncle varies in length from 25 to 100 cm, and the flowers are larger than those of the other two subspecies. The leaves are 4 cm wide.

Agapanthus caulescens subsp. *gracilis*
It was only in 1939 that this subspecies was discovered in open grassland in KwaZulu-Natal. The peduncles are 60 cm in length. The inflorescence bears 20 to 40 flowers, the tips of the petals are clearly curled back. The leaves are 3 cm wide.

Agapanthus coddii PF
Agapanthus coddii is found beside streams and on mountain slopes in the Northern Cape. The species is named after Dr. Codd, who was director of the Botanical Research Institute from 1963 until 1973. He discovered this plant together with Dyer. This deciduous species has an enormous peduncle, 100 to 150 cm in length. The flowers are violet blue and the pollen is purple. The flowering time in its natural habitat is January. The plant enjoys well-drained, fertile soil, sun or light shade and plenty of water in summer.

Agapanthus inapertus PF PV
This, one of the most recognizable species, hails from the southeast of Mpumalanga and the northwest of Swaziland to North. The local inhabitants call the plant "hlakahla". It is a deciduous species and grows in areas where there is abundant rain in open grassland, and in forest clearings and

beside streams. The peduncle varies in length from 30 to 200 cm. The inflorescence consists of 20 to 80 flowers which are erect in bud but pendulous when open. The flowers vary from pale to dark violet blue and only occasionally white. The pollen is yellow. In their natural habitat they flower from December until March.

Agapanthus inapertus subsp. *hollandii* PF
This species occurs in Mpumalanga, where the plant grows in grassland and between rocks. Holland first collected this plant in the areas of Alkmaar and Lydenburg, and the plant was named after him. The flowers are of an extraordinary magenta blue, which makes it one of the most attractive sub-species. The flower segments are shorter than the tube.

Agapanthus inapertus subsp. *inapertus* PF
This subspecies occurs in Mpumalanga and North. The flower is violet blue and occasionally white. The tips of the petals are slightly spread out.

Agapanthus inapertus subsp. *intermedius* (syn. *A. dyeri*) PF PV
This subspecies is found in a very large area and grows in Swaziland, Mpumalanga and North. This plant appears everywhere the species grows, on grassy and rocky mountain slopes and beside streams. The flowers are violet blue. The segments are just as long as the tube. The plant is very variable.

Agapanthus inapertus subsp. *parviflorus* PF
This subspecies grows between blocks of rock in Mpumalanga. The peduncles are 100 cm, and the inflorescence has a diameter of 7 cm and bears 30 to 60 flowers. The flower is very pale violet blue on the inside and pale violet blue on the outside. The segments are narrow.

Agapanthus inapertus subsp. *pendulus* PF PV
This species is found from Belfast and Dullstroom to Lydenburg in Mpumalanga and grows in grassland and on rocky slopes to a height of 2000 m. The peduncle can reach a length of 160 cm. The inflorescence has a diameter of 10 cm and bears 40 flowers. The shade of the flowers varies from dark violet blue to very pale violet blue and is only occasion-

Agapanthus inapertus

Agapanthus praecox subsp. orientalis
(syn. *A. orientalis*) and friends

The stamps read:

The GAMBIA — D3 — Kigelia africana
The GAMBIA — D3 — Hibiscus schizopetalus
The GAMBIA — D3 — Dombeya mastersii
The GAMBIA — D3 — Agapanthus orientalis
The GAMBIA — D3 — Sirelitzia reginae
The GAMBIA — D3 — Spathodea campanulata
The GAMBIA — D3 — Rhodolaena bakeriana
The GAMBIA — D3 — Gazania rigens
The GAMBIA — D3 — Ixianthes retzioides

ally white. The segments are as broad as they are long. Some varieties of this subspecies have the darkest flowers of all *Agapanthus* species and cultivars.

Agapanthus praecox PF PV

This exceptionally variable, evergreen plant occurs in grassy areas, rocky places and alongside the edges of forests in areas of great rainfall. The area in which it is found runs from Port Elizabeth (Eastern Cape) to KwaZulu-Natal. The peduncle is 40 to 150 cm long, and the inflorescence can bear many or few flowers. The funnel-shaped flowers are violet blue or sometimes white; they are not fleshy but have a thin texture. The pollen is yellow. Although two subspecies are recognized it would perhaps be better to consider the species to be extremely variable. In the wild all kinds of variants grow next to each other. This species makes no great demands on its environment, and in its land of origin it is planted in great numbers in parks and gardens. The plants need some moisture in summer but can also grow in very poor soil. In the tropics it can become a troublesome weed that is a threat to local flora.

Agapanthus praecox subsp. *minimus*
(syn. *A. comptonii*) PF PV

This subspecies is found in the Eastern Cape. The peduncle is not as tall as that of the species, some 40 to 100 cm. The inflorescence bears fewer flowers, and they range from pale violet blue to violet blue. The leaf is not broader than 2.5 cm. In other words, a real "minimus".

Agapanthus praecox subsp. *orientalis* PF PV

This subspecies is found in the Eastern Cape and in the south of KwaZulu-Natal. It was already known in France in 1813 and is still grown. The peduncles are 60 to 140 cm in length, and the inflorescence can bear more than 100 flowers. The flowers are pale violet blue to violet blue. The leaf can be up to 5 cm across. This plant is often used in crossbreeding.

Agapanthus praecox subsp. *praecox* PF

This plant is found growing in the wild in the Eastern Cape around Cathcart, Humansdorp and Uitenhage. The peduncle is 80 to 100 cm and bears an inflorescence with many violet blue flowers. The flowers are longer than 5 cm and larger than those of the species.

The determination key for the species (which was compiled by Wim Snoeijer according to Frances Leighton's key and the views of Ben Zonneveld and Graham Duncan) is based on the colour of the pollen, whether the plant is deciduous or evergreen, the width of the leaves and the shape of the flowers. Species can only be true if they have been bred from seed that has been won in its natural habitat. However, it is often the case that seed collected "in the wild" brings forth hybrids. *Agapanthus* is rather promiscuous, and plants cross-breed very easily. Only a few collections contain only species, and seed that has been taken from plants in botanical gardens does not always prove to be true either. It is no wonder that L. H. Bailey, in his *Manual of Cultivated Plants* (1949), gave short shrift to all those hybrids and recognized only one species, *Agapanthus africanus,* which he described as an extremely variable species. He had found a solution for all those crossbreeding plants, but he was wrong. It remains a difficult subject, but thanks to new techniques, things have become clearer and the result is six species and fourteen subspecies.

Two species, *Agapanthus africanus* and *A. caulescens,* received an Award of Garden Merit (AGM) from the Royal Horticultural Society. Snoeijer is of the opinion that a cultivated plant does not represent the species. He believes that a prize should not be awarded to a wild species in the same way as a cultivated species, a cultivar. Species are variable in flower shape, number of flowers per inflorescence, flower colour, etc. Usually only one plant is entered for judging at an exhibition. This one magnificent plant cannot represent the species; and yet, all plants that are sold as *A. africanus* and *A. caulescens,* for instance, even though they are far less attractive than the original prize-winning plants, may bear the same AGM symbol.

Cultivars

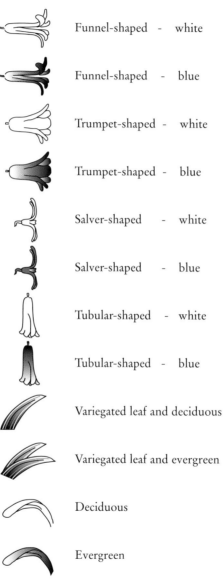

Funnel-shaped   -   white

Funnel-shaped   -   blue

Trumpet-shaped   -   white

Trumpet-shaped   -   blue

Salver-shaped   -   white

Salver-shaped   -   blue

Tubular-shaped   -   white

Tubular-shaped   -   blue

Variegated leaf and deciduous

Variegated leaf and evergreen

Deciduous

Evergreen

From A to Z

From hundreds of cultivars these strong plants have been chosen; they will thrive, providing they are well looked after. These cultivars are to be found at specialized nurseries, even though it may require some searching. The choice of an *Agapanthus* is very personal. Some people prefer a long stem with a huge inflorescence, others appreciate shorter plants. The choice will first of all be between an evergreen or a deciduous plant, and whether it is white or blue. These distinguishing features can be seen at a glance by looking at the symbols accompanying each plant. **(See left).**

Note too that the symbols tell to what group a cultivar belongs (Funnel, Trumpet, etc.). Although *Agapanthus* has been crossbred for more than a century, the classification into five and four groups, respectively, by Gillissen and Snoeijer, has been proved by the DNA research carried out by Zonneveld and Duncan. *Agapanthus africanus* has an extremely high DNA content, which a cultivar never reaches; all cultivars have the same DNA content as the evergreen *A. praecox* or much lower, dropping to that of the deciduous *A. campanulatus* (for breeding new cultivars, *A. campanulatus* and *A. praecox* are usually used).Therefore, a symbol indicates the name of a cultivar's group, instead of a species' name being placed between the genus name and cultivar name.

Not only the size of the leaf, peduncle, inflorescence and flower is noted

Agapanthus 'Albatross'

Agapanthus 'Amsterdam'

(the diameter of a flower is that of the moment when the flower is completely open), but also details of the flower colour. It may seem to be slightly over-doing it to call a flower pale violet blue or dark violet blue, but this is the official designation according to the RHS Colour Chart, which has been specially designed to approach natural colours as closely as possible. The chart consists of 884 colours, each with a name and a number. The colours are grouped together in four fans. Each colour card on a fan has a hole in it so that the card can be placed over a flower or a leaf in order to determine the exact colour; the colour can best be determined in the shade during the middle of the day. Each colour card is made up of four shades. Ordinary blue does not exist when referring to an *Agapanthus* – according to the RHS Colour Chart it is called violet blue. In the following descriptions of the cultivars, only the name of the colour is mentioned, not the number.

This colour chart has a long history in England. Since 1986 the Royal Horticultural Society has been working closely with the Bloemenbureau Holland (Dutch Flower Office) in order to perfect the colour chart still further. The colours used to be given fanciful names like canary yellow and Venetian purple but these have now been replaced by the name of a colour and a number, e.g. violet blue 96D. When this renam-ing was being done, a well-known gar-den journalist expressed his deep sorrow at the disappearance of the old names. He felt that poets had made room for scientists.

Agapanthus 'Albatross'

1976 Oakhurst Nurseries, California, USA

The arching foliage of this white ever-green is dark green with a green base and is 15 to 40 cm long and 2.5 to 3.5 cm wide. The flat peduncle is 80 to 150 cm long (sometimes 40 cm), green and slightly glaucous. The inflorescence, which has a diameter of 18 to 25 cm, consists of 15 to 20 flowers. The inflo-rescence is more or less globular but usually slightly elongated. Flowers emerge from the creamy white, upright flower buds, which are white on the outside and white with a transparent midrib on the inside. When they are fully open, the white flowers are 4 to 4.5 cm long and 4 to 5 cm in diameter. The stamens are exserted and the anthers are yellow. This plant, which hails from the USA, is still being propagated and used as a pot plant but does not appear in the cut flower trade.

Agapanthus 'Amsterdam'

1999 Kees Duivenvoorde, Beverwijk, The Netherlands

The dark green, arching foliage of this dark blue deciduous plant is 30 to 35 cm long and up to 2.4 cm wide; the base is dark violet. The flat, green peduncle is 70 cm long. The globular inflorescence has a diameter of 22 cm and bears 60 flowers. The flower buds are violet blue and upright. The inside of the flower is violet blue with a purple tinge with a purple-tinged violet blue margin. The midrib is rather wide and dark violet blue. The flowers are 4.4 cm long and 4.2 cm in diameter. The stamens are slightly exserted and the anthers are dark violet, turning black later. They are wonderful pot plants but not suitable as cut flowers, due to bud loss.

Agapanthus 'Angela'

2000 Dick Fulcher, GB

Dick Fulcher named this *Agapanthus* after his youngest daughter. The foliage of this pale blue evergreen is 55 to 80 cm in length and 2.2 to 3 cm broad. The 120-cm-long peduncle bears a more or less tubular inflorescence 17 cm in diameter. The flower buds are pale violet blue and the flowers are violet blue on the inside and paler in colour on the outside. The midrib is slightly darker. The flowers are 3.4 cm long and 3.5 cm in diameter. The stamens are only slightly exserted or not at all and the anthers are black.

Agapanthus 'Ardernei'

1966

It is not known who was responsible for breeding this plant, but 'Ardernei' was

first shown in England at an exhibition of the Royal Horticultural Society in 1966. The leaves of this white deciduous plant are 30 to 50 cm in length and 2.5 cm wide, slightly glaucous and purple at the base. The flat peduncle is 60 to 100 cm long and green flushed purple. The more or less tubular inflorescence has a diameter of 15 cm and bears 30 to 60, sometimes 20 to 80 flowers. When the flowers open they are white on the inside with a transparent midrib and white with very pale purple on the outside. The flowers are 2.5 to 3 cm long and 2.5 to 3 cm in diameter. The stamens do not protrude and the anthers are black. This plant is usually propagated from seed, and it would be better to consider the name as referring to a group of similar plants rather than to a cultivar. However, although the plants that bear this name are somewhat varied, they resemble each other enough to give them the cultivar name. The white *Agapanthus* in the famous garden at

Sissinghurst (GB) is most probably 'Ardernei'.

Agapanthus 'Argenteus Vittatus'

This variegated cultivar has been known since 1865 and is still being propagated. On the island of Madeira this plant is very common and is generally to be seen standing on a staircase or beside the front door. The evergreen foliage is 3 cm wide and 30 cm in length and has white stripes. However, when grown in a container the leaves will not be so large. The plant does not flower well and, most usually, not at all. The flowers when they appear are pale violet blue with exserted stamens. The plant does not bear fruit.

Agapanthus 'Aureovittatus'

This variegated cultivar has been known in The Netherlands since 1875 and since

Agapanthus 'Aureovittatus'

Agapanthus 'Black Beauty'

Agapanthus 'Blue Giant'

1885 in England. The evergreen leaves are longer but narrower than those of 'Argenteus Vittatus' and have a yellow margin with green stripes in the centre, which fade to pale yellow. This cultivar flowers better than most of the variegated plants but not profusely. A flowering 'Aureovittatus' was exhibited in the Artis Zoo in Amsterdam in 1891.

Agapanthus 'Beth Chatto'

Considering the name this would seem to be a young cultivar, but this variegated plant has been known in England since 1865. However, the plants are sold at the nursery in the Beth Chatto Gardens in England. Most variegated plants are evergreens but this one is deciduous, with foliage from 15 cm in length and 1 cm across. The leaves have narrow yellow stripes which later become greener. The flowers are violet blue.

Agapanthus 'Black Beauty'

1997 Kees Duivenvoorde, Beverwijk, The Netherlands

This dark blue deciduous plant has leaves that are 25 cm in length and 2 cm across. The leaves are dark green, somewhat glaucous and have a purple base. The flat peduncle is 40 to 60 cm long, dark violet blue with only the base green. The globular inflorescence has a diameter of 15 to 17 cm and bears 40 to 60 flowers. The flower stems are very dark violet blue. The flower bud is dark violet blue and upright at first but quickly becomes horizontal. The flower is pale violet blue on the inside with a darker margin. The three inner petals are almost white at the base and the midrib is violet blue. The outside of the petals is violet blue whilst the midrib and the base are dark violet blue. The flowers are 3.5 cm long and 2.3 cm in diameter. The stamens are not exserted and the anthers are black. This *Agapanthus* owes its name to the wonderful black seed heads that appear after flowering and make the plant especially attractive.

Agapanthus 'Blue Giant'

1951 J. K. Zandberg, The Netherlands

This pale blue evergreen has upright to arching leaves that vary in colour from pale to normal green, are glaucous and have a green base. The flat peduncle is 80 to 120 cm, sometimes even 150 cm long. The globular inflorescence has a diameter of 17 to 23 cm and bears 90 to 130 flowers. Pale violet blue flowers appear from the upright violet blue buds. They are almost white at the base and flushed with purple at the tip. The midrib is darker. The flowers are 4 to 4.5 cm in length and 2.5 to 3.5 in diameter. The stamens are not exserted and the anthers are violet. Suitable as a pot plant but unsuitable as a cut flower because the plant does not produce many flowers.

Agapanthus 'Blue Globe'

1964 Hoogervorst, Oegstgeest, The Netherlands

This blue evergreen has 30- to 60-cm-long, upright leaves that are green to dark green, slightly glaucous and green at the base. The distinctly flat peduncle is 80 to 120 cm, slightly glaucous and green. It supports a globular inflorescence with a diameter of 15 to 22 cm, bearing 80 to 100 flowers. The buds are upright and violet blue with a darker base and green tip. The flowers are violet blue on the inside with a purple tinged margin. The stamens are not exserted and the anthers are yellow tinged with violet. The first flowers to appear often have 8 petals. This cultivar, which was selected from seedlings, is difficult to obtain.

Agapanthus 'Blue Heaven'

1999 C. J. de Jong & A. Ph. M. Rijnbeek and Son, Boskoop, The Netherlands

European Plant Breeders Right applied for and granted. This blue deciduous plant is of recent date. The arching foliage is 40 cm in length and 3 cm across. It is light green to green and has a green base. The round, green peduncle is 70 to 80 cm long and bears a more or less flat inflorescence that is 16 cm in diameter with 30 to 50 flowers. The flower bud is violet blue and the flower is purple flushed violet blue on the inside with a darker violet blue midrib. The flowers are 4.2 to 4.4 cm in length and 5 cm in diameter. The stamens are exserted and have dark violet blue anthers that later turn black.

Agapanthus 'Blue Moon'

1987 Eric Smith, Buckshaw Gardens, Holwell, Dorset GB

This slow-growing and late-flowering plant also takes a long time before it flowers. But the unusual greyish blue colour of the flowers is well worth the wait. Although the plant has only been known since 1987, it is probably much older. The evergreen foliage is 30 to 50 cm in length and 3.5 cm wide, is upright and glossy green with a green base. The sturdy peduncle is 70 to 90 cm long, green and glaucous. The flat inflorescence has a diameter of 12 to 14 cm and bears 50 flowers. An outstanding feature is that the bract does not drop off. The buds are violet blue with creamy white tips and a slightly darker base. The flowers are violet blue on the inside with a slightly darker midrib and mar-

Agapanthus 'Blue Globe'

Agapanthus 'Blue Heaven'

Agapanthus 'Blue Moon'

gin. The outside of the flower is pale violet blue but the base is darker. The stamens are not exserted and the anther is dark violet.

Agapanthus 'Blue Triumphator'

1916. A very old cultivar, probably of Dutch origin

Most plants on sale under this name nowadays have been propagated from seed, and the true cultivar is rare. It would be preferable to designate the name as a group name. This name would then be used for a group of plants that have been propagated by seed and resemble each other but are not the true cultivar. The foliage of this blue decidu-ous plant is 30 to 60 cm in length (some-times longer or shorter) and 1.5 to 2 cm (sometimes 4 cm) wide. The leaf is upright, green and glaucous with a slightly paler green base. The rather slender, round peduncle is 70 to 120 cm long and bears a globular, loose inflores-cence with a diameter of 12 to 15 cm and 50 to 70 flowers (or fewer). The vio-let blue bud has a brownish tip and a darker base. The colour of the flower, which is called grey, is officially violet blue on the inside and violet blue with a purple flushed midrib on the inside. The stamens are not exserted and the anthers are dark violet. Because of the slender stalks, which blow all over the place, the plant is not recommended for the gar-den. This old cultivar, which has been followed by new and better examples, is still used for breeding. The new cultivars 'Stockholm', 'Helsinki', and 'Oslo' somewhat resemble 'Blue Triumphator'.

Agapanthus 'Blue Velvet'

1993 Dick Fulcher, GB

The leaves of this blue deciduous *Agapanthus* are 30 to 60 cm in length and 2 to 2.7 cm wide. The dark green flat peduncles are 75 to 120 cm long and each bears a tubular inflorescence 20 cm in diameter, with 50 flowers. The flow-ers are 4.2 cm long and 3.6 cm in diame-ter. The inside is pale violet blue and the outside is violet blue with a purple tinge. The midrib is quite wide. The stamens are not exserted and the anthers are dark violet. According to the breeder, this cultivar resembles 'Purple Cloud' but is not as tall.

Agapanthus 'Blue Triumphator'

Agapanthus **'Bressingham Blue'**

1972 Alan Bloom, Bressingham Gardens, Diss, Norfolk, GB

Bloom, from the well-known English nursery Bressingham Gardens, sowed a large number of *Agapanthus* seed in about 1960. This resulted in 1967 in a bed of more than 2000 flowering seedlings. From these he selected the nine most beautiful and planted them close to his home. After a further two years of growing these nine plants were still identical, and he decided to propagate them. In ten years' time there were more than 1000 plants, which were offered in his catalogue as 'Bressingham Blue'. This dark blue deciduous plant has foliage that is 30 to 40 cm in length and 2 cm wide, arching, glossy green, and also green at the base. The round peduncle is 80 to 90 cm in length (or shorter), green, slightly glaucous and purple close to the inflorescence. The

flat inflorescence is not large, 12 cm across, and consists of 40 flowers. The dark violet blue flower bud is upright, but soon starts to droop. The flower is violet blue with purple on the inside with a darker margin and still darker midrib. The stamens are not protruding and the anthers are violet blue. An attractive plant for the garden but not for the cut flower grower because there is no demand for drooping flowers. Because the inflorescence is not large, this profusely flowering plant combines well with other garden plants.

Agapanthus **'Bressingham White'**

1972 Alan Bloom, Bressingham Gardens, Diss, Norfolk, GB

In the same flower bed where the 2000 seedlings were growing, from which 'Bressingham Blue' was selected, there were a few white-flowering plants. One of these was selected and named. The

leaf of this white deciduous plant is, with its 30 cm length, somewhat shorter than its blue counterpart, but it is also 2 cm wide. The peduncles are considerably longer, 80 to 100 cm, and flat instead of round. The flat inflorescence is slightly larger – 15 cm – and bears more flowers, about 40 to 50. On the inside of the flower a transparent midrib can be seen, and the white flower has a pale purple apex on the outside. The flowers are 3 cm long and 2.5 cm across. The stamens are not exserted and the anthers are black.

Agapanthus **'Bristol'**

1999 Kees Duivenvoorde, Beverwijk, The Netherlands

A dark blue deciduous plant which has 40 cm long, dark green, slightly arching leaves; dark violet at the base. The leaf is 2.5 cm wide. The flat, 90-cm-long, green peduncles have dark violet speckles. The large 17-cm-wide globular inflores-

Agapanthus 'Castle of Mey' *Agapanthus* 'Catharina' *Agapanthus* 'Cobalt Blue'

cences bear more than 70 flowers. Dark violet flowers emerge from the very dark violet flower buds, and have even darker midribs. The stamens are not exserted and the anthers are violet blue. The flowers are 2.2 to 2.8 cm in length and 1.8 to 2.2 cm across.

Agapanthus 'Castle of Mey'

1975 The Crown Estate, Windsor, GB

This cultivar was named after the castle in Scotland that was bought by Lady Elizabeth Bowes-Lyon, the Queen Mother (1900–2002). She renovated the castle and spent a few weeks during the summer months there for 50 years. She bought the castle because she had spent her childhood in Scotland; it was the only house she owned. She donated the castle and the 20 hectares estate to a foundation, to ensure that it would be retained. This pale blue, deciduous *Agapanthus* has fairly short (15 to 30

cm) and fairly narrow (1 to 1.5 cm) leaves. The round peduncles have adapted themselves and are 60 to 75 cm in length. The more or less flat inflorescence, 12 to 14 cm, bears 40 to 60 flowers. The flowers are violet blue on the inside and pale violet blue with a purple tinge on the outside. They are 3.2 cm in length and 3 to 3.5 cm in diameter. The dark violet stamens are exserted.

Agapanthus 'Catharina'

1995 Kees Duivenvoorde, Beverwijk, The Netherlands

The breeder Kees Duivenvoorde named this *Agapanthus* after his wife and daughter, both of whom are called Catharina. This dark blue, deciduous plant has upright leaves, the tops of which are curled back, and measure 35 cm. The leaf is 3.5 cm wide. The flat green peduncle, which is speckled purple, is 90 cm in length. The globular inflorescence has a diameter of 20 to 23

cm and bears 50 to 70 flowers. The buds are violet blue, and the first flowers have more than the normal number of tepals, 6 to 8 and sometimes even 10. The inside of the flower is pale violet blue with a darker midrib and the outside is the same colour but with a darker base. The flowers are 3.5 cm long and 3 to 3.5 cm in diameter. The stamens are slightly exserted and the anthers are dark violet. 'Catharina' flowers early in the season.

Agapanthus 'Cobalt Blue'

1988 Beth Chatto, Elmstead Market, GB

This blue deciduous plant, selected by the well-known Beth Chatto, is a beautiful, profusely flowering cultivar. Wim Snoeijer and Chatto had an exchange of letters about the name of this cultivar, because previously the name of a cultivar was not allowed to be related to its colour. Snoeijer acquainted her with this fact and asked her if she would let him

Agapanthus 'Columba' *Agapanthus* 'Copenhagen'

know if she changed the name; if he heard nothing from her, he would call the plant 'Beth Chatto'. "What a mouthful and fairly meaningless!" was her reaction in her letter. Happily for Beth Chatto, the rules have been changed, and colours are now allowed to be used in a cultivar name. 'Cobalt Blue' is now accepted as the correct name. At the present time a variegated *Agapanthus* that is sold at her nursery is called 'Beth Chatto'. 'Cobalt Blue' has 40- to 50-cm-long upright leaves and a round, green peduncle that is tinged purple towards the inflorescence and is 80 to 120 cm long. The more or less globular inflorescence has a diameter of 11 to 13 cm and bears 25 to 40 flowers. The flower is violet blue on the inside with a darker midrib and the outside is violet blue, tinged purple. The flowers are both 3

cm long and across. The stamens are not exserted and the anthers are purple violet at first, later turning black.

Agapanthus 'Columba'

1995 Kees Duivenvoorde, Beverwijk, The Netherlands

Duivenvoorde named this early-flowering plant after his sister. Her name is Duif ("dove"), translated into Latin, *columba*. Duif Duivenvoorde, who as a nun is called Sister Columba, takes a great interest in the flowers her brother breeds. This dark blue deciduous plant has leaves that are 40 cm long, 3 cm wide and upright. The flat peduncle is 70 cm long and green with purple speckles. The globular inflorescence has a diameter of 18 cm and bears 70 flowers. The buds are dark violet blue. The

flowers are 4 cm long and 3.5 cm across, the inside is paler in colour than the outside and the midrib is darker. The stamens are not exserted and the anthers are dark violet. 'Columba' flowers early and is an excellent cut flower. The flower is in great demand because the flower is dark blue. This early flowerer is also suitable for the garden.

Agapanthus 'Copenhagen'

2002 Kees Duivenvoorde, Beverwijk, The Netherlands

This new, dark blue deciduous plant has been specially selected for its late flowering time. The peduncle grows to 100 cm and has a tubular inflorescence 15 cm in diameter. The inflorescence bears 50 flowers which are a fairly uniform shade of dark violet blue.

Agapanthus 'Donau'

Agapanthus 'Dr Brouwer'

Agapanthus 'Duivenbrugge White'

Agapanthus '**Donau**'

1979 W. Schoehuys, Uitgeest, The Netherlands

This plant created a revolution upon its introduction because it produced so many flowers. For many years this cultivar was grown as a cut flower, but it has now been overtaken by other plants. It is still available as a pot plant. This dark blue deciduous plant was named after the River Danube, or Donau as it is called in The Netherlands. The leaves are 30 cm long and 2 to 2.5 cm wide. The flat, green slightly glaucous peduncles are 60 to 80 cm in length. They each carry an inflorescence that measures 15 to 20 cm across and has 40 to 60 (sometimes 20) flowers. The buds are violet blue. The flower measures 3.5 cm in length and 3 cm across. The inside is paler violet blue than the outside, the stamens are not exserted and the anther is dark violet.

Agapanthus '**Dr Brouwer**'

1987 Kees Duivenvoorde, Beverwijk, The Netherlands

This pale blue deciduous plant was the first cultivar that Kees Duivenvoorde registered. He named it after Dr T. Brouwer, a specialist in the hospital in Heemskerk in the province of North Holland. The leaf measures 30 to 40 cm in length and is 2 cm wide. The round, 80-cm-long peduncle is green and dark purple towards the top. The globular inflorescence has a diameter of 19 cm and bears 50 flowers. Both the inside and the outside of the flower are pale purple violet with a darker midrib. The flowers are 4 to 4.4 cm long and 3.5 to 4 cm across. The stamens are not exserted and the anthers are dark violet. This is the most popular cultivar for the cut flower industry, beloved for its dark buds. The flowers are sold when in bud. When they open they are slightly paler. Great numbers of 'Dr Brouwer' can be seen at florists' in August.

Agapanthus '**Duivenbrugge White**'

1998 Kees Duivenvoorde, Beverwijk, The Netherlands

This white seedling from 'Prinses Marilène' got its name from a compilation of the breeder's name, Kees Duivenvoorde, and his wife's name, Catharina Verbrugge. The 90-cm-long peduncles of this white deciduous plant are more or less round. They bear a globular inflorescence which is 12 cm in diameter and consists of 50 flowers. The flower bud is greenish white and has a green stem. The flower is white with a yellowish white midrib on the inside and white with a very pale cream midrib on the outside. The flowers are 2.5 to 2.7 cm long and have a diameter of 3.4 cm; the anthers are yellow.

Agapanthus 'Elisabeth'

1996 Kees Duivenvoorde, Beverwijk, The Netherlands

This cultivar was named after the breeder's daughter. The foliage of this blue deciduous plant is 30 to 40 cm long, 2.5 cm wide, slightly arching and dark green. The flat peduncle is 90 cm long, green flushed purple. The globular inflorescence has a diameter of 17 cm and consists of 60 flowers. The inside of the flower is pale violet blue flushed purple, has a slightly darker margin and a darker midrib. The outside is slightly darker, just as the midrib. The flower is 3.4 cm long and 2.5 to 3 cm in diameter. The stamens are not exserted and the anthers are violet at first, later turning to black.

Agapanthus 'Ellamae'

1990 Los Angeles State and County Arboretum, California, USA

Now there's a plant with a good southern name! (American catalogue)
The leaves of this pale blue evergreen are 60 cm long and 4.5 cm wide. This American cultivar has a huge inflorescence but the flowers are, in comparison, small. The round peduncle, 90 to 130 cm in length, has a globular inflorescence, with a diameter of 22 cm, which bears 100 to 150 flowers. The inside of the flower is pale violet blue with a white base and the outside is violet blue. The midrib is dark violet blue. The stamens are slightly exserted, the anthers are violet blue with yellow pollen. This plant is U.S. Plant Patent no. 7297. The opinions of experts about this cultivar are divided. Some do not think the plant has a right to a patent because the individual flowers are small; others have never seen such a beautiful plant.

Agapanthus 'Flore Pleno'

1878 France

This blue evergreen was probably discovered in France in 1878. The plant has been known in England since 1885 and from 1888 in The Netherlands. The leaves are 25 cm in length and 2 cm wide and the round peduncle is 80 cm long and green with purple speckles. The inflorescence is 18 cm in diameter and bears 30 flowers. The flower bud is violet blue. The flower itself is violet blue flushed purple, both on the inside and the outside, and it has a darker midrib. The flowers are 4 to 4.5 cm long and 4 cm across. The stamens and the pistil have changed into segment-like stamin-

Agapanthus 'Elisabeth'

Agapanthus 'Ellamae'

Agapanthus 'Flore Pleno'

odes, which makes the flowers appear to be double. As this is the only double-flowered cultivar it ought to be in every collection. The buds do not always open.

Agapanthus 'Franni'

2004 Beth Chatto, Elmstead Market, Colchester, GB

This plant was named after the editor of the American publishing firm Timber Press who edited Wim Snoeijer's book *Agapanthus: A Revision of the Genus*. Whilst writing his book, Wim Snoeijer came to the conclusion that this plant, which was bred under the name *Agapanthus campanulatus* 'Albidus' at the Beth Chatto Gardens, was a separate clone and deserved a cultivar name. 'Franni' is a white, deciduous plant with leaves that are 30 to 40 cm long and 2 cm wide. The round peduncles are 50 to 100 cm in length. The inflorescence has a diameter of 6 to 11 cm and is com-

posed of 30 to 50 flowers. The flowers are white with a touch of pale purple, 2 to 2.5 cm long and 2 cm across. The stamens are slightly exserted and the anthers are black.

Agapanthus 'Gayle's Lilac'

1997 New Zealand

This blue evergreen *Agapanthus* is an exceptionally popular plant and common in the trade. The peduncle, 40 to 50 cm in length, bears an inflorescence with 30 to 40 flowers. The flowers are very pale violet, almost white, and have a violet midrib.

Agapanthus 'Glacier Stream'

1995 Maas & van Stein, Hillegom, The Netherlands

This white deciduous cultivar has been on the market for years under the name WitC. It was only in 1995 that the plant

was introduced under the name 'Glacier Stream'. 'Glacier Stream' is often mixed up with 'Polar Ice', also white and from the same breeder, although there are very clear differences. The leaves of 'Glacier Stream' are green and twice as long as those of 'Polar Ice', whilst the leaves of the latter are purple at the base. The peduncle of 'Glacier Stream' is flat, green with purple and 100 cm in length, whilst that of 'Polar Ice' is green, round and measures 60 to 80 cm. The flat inflorescence of 'Glacier Stream' is 15 cm in diameter and bears 50 to 60 flowers, whilst the inflorescence of 'Polar Ice' is smaller, 12 to 15 cm, but bears more flowers, 60 to 80. The flower stem of 'Glacier Stream' is greenish purple and that of 'Polar Ice' is green. The flower of 'Glacier Stream' is white on the inside, with a transparent midrib, and tinged with violet on the outside, whilst the 'Polar Ice' flower is white with a yellowish apex. The size of the individual flowers differs little. The sta-

mens of both flowers are not exserted but 'Glacier Stream' has black anthers and 'Polar Ice' yellow. In general, 'Polar Ice' gives a whiter impression than 'Glacier Stream' but neither plant is pure white.

Agapanthus 'Glen Avon'

1997 A. D. Gray, Glen Avon, New Plymouth, New Zealand

The cultivar name of this *Agapanthus* is usually wrongly rendered 'Glenavon'. The evergreen leaf is rather wide and the 100-cm-long peduncle has a globular inflorescence, with a diameter of 20 cm, which can bear up to 350 flowers. The flowers usually have 10 instead of 6 tepals. They are violet blue with a darker midrib and the stamens are not exserted . This cultivar was first introduced as 'Fragrant Glen' but when the flowers turned out to be less fragrant than had been expected, it was renamed 'Glen Avon'.

Agapanthus 'Goldfinger'

2001 Kees Duivenvoorde, Beverwijk, The Netherlands

The foliage of this variegated *Agapanthus* is more or less evergreen. The leaves are 20 cm long and 0.9 cm wide. They are pale green with yellow stripes and have a wide yellow margin. They usually lie flat on the ground. This spontaneous mutation does not flower: Kees Duivenvoorde, the breeder, has not seen one flower in ten years.

Agapanthus 'Graskop'

1987 Botanical Garden, Kirstenbosch, South Africa

This cultivar is a selection from *Agapanthus inapertus* subsp. *pendulus* and originates from the region around Graskop in Mpumalanga. This dark blue deciduous plant has leaves that are 40 cm long and 3.8 cm wide and round peduncles 80 to 150 cm in length. The drooping inflorescence is small, 12 cm in diameter, and bears 30 to 40 pendulous flowers. They are 4.7 cm long and 1.5 cm across. The inside of the flower is pale violet blue with a darker margin and the outside is dark purple blue. As this plant is often on offer as seed the colour varies considerably. Today 'Graskop' is propagated by micropropagation and should, therefore, have good colour, providing the correct basic material is used. In 2002, Hans Kramer from the Hessenhof introduced 'Graskopje', a seedling of 'Graskop', which is much smaller than the parent plant.

Agapanthus 'Graskop'

Agapanthus Headbourne Hybrids

Agapanthus plants that are sold nowadays as Headbourne Hybrids all fall under the category RUBBISH. This does not only apply to the name Headbourne Hybrids, but also to 'Headbourne A', 'Headbourne Blue', 'Headbourne White', etc. Originally the Headbourne Hybrids were a group of plants bred by Lewis Palmer, an Englishman who lived in Winchester, Hampshire, GB. After visiting the Botanical Garden at Kirstenbosch in South Africa, he asked if they would send him some *Agapanthus* seed. From this seed he bred 300 seedlings and discovered that they were all hybrids. The ancestry of the seed has never been completely clarified. It is highly probable that the seed was from *Agapanthus campanulatus* and also from *A. inapertus*

and *A. praecox*. Between 1950 and 1960 Palmer selected and named many plants from these original seedlings such as 'Lady Grey' (1951). In 1963 he also collected seed himself in South Africa. Palmer was an authority on *Agapanthus*. He has greatly contributed to the popularity of the *Agapanthus* in England and propagated them in his own garden, Headbourne Worthy Grange in Hampshire. The Headbourne Hybrids are named after his garden. The original plants, which were introduced by Palmer as Headbourne Hybrids (also called Palmer Hybrids), are still growing in the gardens of Howick Hall, Alnwick, Northumberland, in the north of England. The garden is now part of a foundation that is managed by Lord Howick, who is the son of Lady Mary Howick. Lewis Palmer was the brother of Lady Grey. Lady Grey, after which an *Agapanthus* was named, was Lady Mary Howick's mother. The original Headbourne Hybrids, which grow in the garden on the second terrace of Howick Hall, transform this terrace into a wonderful sea of blue at the back end of the summer.

It is a great pity that the plants now sold as Headbourne Hybrids are so disappointing. These plants have little or absolutely nothing in common with the original Headbourne Hybrids from Lewis Palmer. Everything that is propagated through seed is, without any selection, sold under the name Headbourne Hybrids because the name is known and plants bearing this name sell well. You have been warned. Do not buy these plants because they could be just about anything.

Agapanthus **'Hinag'** SUMMER GOLD

1986 Ramon Alaniz Mendoza, Santa Ana, California, USA

This plant is a seedling of 'Peter Pan'. It is notable in that it is a profusely flowering, variegated plant. The evergreen leaves, which are 42 cm long and 2 cm wide, are green with yellow stripes and have a yellow margin. The peduncle is 45 to 60 cm long and is green and yellow. The inflorescence has a diameter of 10.5 cm and bears 50 violet blue flowers. The stamens are not exserted and the anthers are yellow.

Agapanthus **'Ice Lolly'**

1995 Maas & van Stein, Hillegom, The Netherlands

'Ice Lolly' is one of the white trio from Maas & van Stein. The other two are 'Glacier Stream' and 'Polar Ice'. The leaves of this white deciduous plant are 30 to 40 cm long and 2.5 cm wide. The round peduncle is 80 to 100 cm long and has a tubular inflorescence that is 18 cm in diameter. It bears 80 flowers. The inside of the flower, which is 3 to 3.5 cm long and 3.5 to 4 cm across, is white with a transparent midrib. The outside is also white but here the midrib is pale yellow at the apex. The stamens are not exserted and the anthers are yellow.

Agapanthus **'Intermedius'**

1946

This old, deciduous cultivar is still being grown as a cut flower and is called 'Intermedia' by the growers.

'Intermedius' was already known in 1887, when it was described in Leichtlin's catalogue in Germany. Since 1920 this plant has been on offer in van Tubergen's catalogue. In 1946 van Tubergen also had an 'Intermedius' in its catalogue. The two descriptions are, however, different. Probably the plants that are still on offer under this name are from the 1946 van Tubergen plants. The plant that is now known in the nurseries as 'Intermedia' should really be given a new name to avoid further confusion. Moreover, the cultivar name does not comply with the rules. The leaves of 'Intermedius' are 20 to 30 cm in length and 1.8 cm wide. The round peduncle is 70 cm long and has a more or less flat inflorescence which is 14 cm in diameter. The buds are very dark violet blue. The flowers are violet blue on the inside with a slightly darker midrib and on the outside dark violet blue with an even darker midrib. The flowers are 2.5 to 3 cm in length and 2 to 3 cm across. The stamens are not exserted and they have dark violet anthers. If large clumps of *Agapanthus* are on sale at plant shows then this will usually be 'Intermedius'. The bulb merchants buy these plants from nurserymen who have had them in the soil for about 10 to 15 years. Such a large plant looks tempting but will never flower, so buying it is to be discouraged.

Agapanthus 'Intermedius'

Agapanthus 'Isis'

1955 Alan Bloom, Bressingham Gardens, Diss, Norfolk, GB

Bloom named this deciduous cultivar 'Isis' because of its deep blue colour. Under this name two different clones are propagated, which can cause confusion. The "real" 'Isis' has leaves 40 cm in length and 1.5 to 2 cm wide. The round, green peduncle is 75 to 100 cm long and the flat inflorescence, which is 12 cm in diameter, bears 40 to 50 flowers. The buds are dark violet. The flowers are violet blue fading to white at the base on the inside with a darker midrib and a slightly darker purple margin. The outside is violet blue with a purple apex and midrib and a darker base. The flowers are 2.5 cm long and 2.5 cm across. The stamens are not exserted and have purplish yellow anthers.

Agapanthus 'Jack's Blue'

2001 New Zealand

This blue evergreen got its name from the well-known nurseryman, Jack Blythe, from New Zealand. The plant has peduncles 120 to 150 cm in length and enormous inflorescences 25 cm in diameter. The buds are dark violet blue and the flowers violet blue with green anthers. The contrast between the colour of the buds and the open flowers is large. The plant strongly resembles 'Purple Cloud' but the flowers are larger.

Agapanthus 'Jodie'

2000 Dick Fulcher, Pine Cottage Plants, Fourways, GB

This evergreen plant, named after the youngest granddaughter of the breeder, has a peduncle 140 to 150 cm in length. The violet blue flowers have a darker midrib. The stamens are not exserted and the anther is violet. The plant flowers late.

Agapanthus 'Lady Grey'

1951 Lewis Palmer, GB

Lady Grey was the sister of Lewis Palmer, the well-known *Agapanthus* man. This greyish blue deciduous plant is especially popular in England. The leaves are 40 to 50 cm in length and 1.5 cm wide. The round peduncle is 50 to 85 cm long and bears a round inflorescence with a diameter of 10 to 13 cm and 40 flowers. A violet blue flower appears from the dark violet bud and it has a white base on the inside. The midrib and the base of the outside of the flower petals are darker. The flowers are 2.5 cm long and just as wide in diameter. The stamens are not exserted and the anthers are violet. This cultivar is also known in the trade under the (wrong) name 'Mabel Grey'.

Agapanthus 'Lady Moore'

In 1960 Elizabeth Perker Jervis introduced this cultivar, which had been
found in the garden of Miss Raphael in
Kingston Bagpize, GB. The plant is
named after Lady Phyllis Moore, wife of
Sir Frederick Moore, who was director
of the Botanical Gardens in Glasnevin in
Ireland until 1922. She was known as an
excellent gardener and plantswoman.
This white deciduous plant has rather
narrow foliage, 1.5 cm wide, and 40 cm
in length. The round peduncle, 40 to 70
cm in length, has a flat inflorescence 12
cm in diameter consisting of 10 to 40
flowers. The flowers are 2.5 cm long and
the same in diameter. They are white
with a transparent midrib. The three
outside tepals have a violet apex. The
stamens are not exserted and the anthers
are dark purplish violet. This cultivar
with its attractive small, white, round
clusters shows that the inflorescences do
not need to be large to be beautiful.

Agapanthus 'Leicester'

1999 Kees Duivenvoorde, Beverwijk, The Netherlands

This white deciduous plant is one of the
"town series" raised by Duivenvoorde.
The plant is similar to 'Spalding', which
was introduced one year earlier, but it
has a shorter peduncle. The somewhat
flat peduncle, which is 60 to 70 cm long,
has a flat inflorescence of 15 to 17 cm,
bearing 40 to 70 flowers. The creamy
white flower bud is flushed light purple
at the apex. The flower is 4 cm long and
4.7 cm in diameter, is white on the inside
and has a narrow, transparent midrib.
The flower is white on the outside with
a pale purple apex. The stamens are
exserted and have purple anthers.

Agapanthus 'Liam's Lilac'

1997 Dick Fulcher, Pine Cottage Plants, Fourways, GB

It is clear from the name what the
colour of this deciduous plant is,
although the official colour is purple
violet. Dick Fulcher named this
Agapanthus after his eldest grandson.
The peduncle is 80 to 100 cm.

Agapanthus 'Lilac Time'

1993 Dick Fulcher, Bicton College, Devon, GB

This blue evergreen has peduncles that are 90 to 125 cm in length. The tubular inflorescence is 19 cm in diameter and bears 60 to 70 flowers. The flowers are pale violet blue with a slightly darker midrib and are 3.2 to 3.5 long. When the flowers are completely open the segments curl backwards. The stamens are not exserted and the anther is blue at first, later brown.

Agapanthus 'Lilliput'

1950 Roland Jackman, Woking, GB

This profusely flowering, dark blue deciduous plant serves its name well. The leaf is 10 to 20 cm long and 0.3 to 1.2 cm wide. The round peduncles are 20 to 60 cm long and have a flat inflorescence, with a diameter of 10 cm, which bears 20 to 25 flowers. The flower is dark violet blue on the inside and the midrib is darker. The outside is dark violet blue with a slightly darker base. The stamens are exserted and the anthers are violet. Because the plant is so small, qualities of "ordinary" perennials are attributed to it. It is said to be fully winter hardy, but this is not true. This cultivar needs a winter cover, too.

Agapanthus 'Loch Hope' AGM

1974 The Crown Estate, Windsor, GB

This blue deciduous *Agapanthus* was named after a lake in Scotland. The dark green leaves are upright, 30 to 50 cm long and 3 cm wide. The round, not too sturdy, peduncle can reach a length of 60 to 100 cm, sometimes even 150 cm, and is green with purple. The flat inflorescence has a diameter of 12 to 16 cm and bears 50 to 70 flowers. The flower is 3.8 cm long and 3.5 to 4 cm in diameter. The inside of the flower is violet blue with a darker midrib and margin. The outside is purple tinged at the base. The stamens are not exserted and the anther is dark violet. This is one of the most popular tall *Agapanthus* plants, partly due to the dark blue colour and the pendulous flowers. However, this late-flowering plant is not interesting for the cut flower trade because of its pendulous flowers. Plants which have been raised from seed are also offered under this name, and they do not always possess the same characteristics. Buy plants that have been vegetatively propagated at a good nursery. 'Loch Hope' is the only cultivar that has been crowned with an Award of Garden Merit (AGM).

Agapanthus 'Lilac Time'

Agapanthus 'Lilliput'

Agapanthus 'Loch Hope'

Agapanthus 'Marianne'

Agapanthus 'Mariètte'

Agapanthus 'Meibont'

Agapanthus 'Marianne'

1987 Kees Duivenvoorde, Beverwijk, The Netherlands

This blue deciduous plant was named after Marianne Hendriks, a friend of the breeder. The leaves are 20 cm in length and 2.5 cm wide. The exceptionally sturdy, round peduncle is 50 cm long and the globular inflorescence, with its diameter of 17 cm, bears 60 to 90 flowers. The flower is 4.5 cm long and 4 cm in diameter and is pale violet blue with a violet blue midrib and a purple tinged margin. The outside is pale violet blue with a darker midrib and base. The stamens are not exserted and the anthers are violet. This sturdy plant, with it lovely foliage and large clusters of flowers, is suitable for both container cultivation and also as a cut flower. The flower clusters are almost as large as those of an evergreen *Agapanthus*.

Agapanthus 'Mariètte'

1988 Kees Duivenvoorde, Beverwijk, The Netherlands

This blue deciduous plant has been specially selected for its late flowering. The dark green leaves are 25 to 30 cm long and 1.8 cm wide and the strong, flat peduncles are 40, sometimes 60, cm long. The tubular inflorescence has a diameter of 14 cm and bears 80 flowers. The flower bud is first pale green with a violet blue apex and later turns to pale violet blue with a darker apex. The flowers are 3 to 3.5 cm long and 2.9 cm in diameter. The inside is pale violet blue with a violet blue midrib and a slightly purple tinged margin. The outside is pale violet blue flushed purple and darker toward the apex. The stamens are exserted and the anthers are black.

Agapanthus 'Meibont'

1998 Hans Kramer, De Hessenhof Nursery, Ede, The Netherlands

This cultivar from Hans Kramer lives up to its name and is only variegated in the month of May. The more or less deciduous leaves, which are 40 cm in length and 2.3 cm in diameter, are at that time of the year half green and half creamy yellow. In the summer they turn green with a yellow tip or completely green. Because the plant is not always variegated, it is not classified as a variegated cultivar. 'Meibont' has 50 to 60 violet blue flowers, which are clustered together in an inflorescence 15 cm in diameter. The peduncle is 80 cm long.

Agapanthus 'Midnight Blue'

1976 Philip Wood, Slieve Donard Nursery, Newcastle, County Down, Northern Ireland

This dark blue, low-growing deciduous plant was attained from seed that Philip Wood was sent from South Africa. The thin, green peduncle, which is 30 cm long, is flushed violet at the top. The inflorescence has 20 flowers, each with a diameter of 1.5 cm. The flowers are dark violet blue on the inside with a white base and the outside is dark violet blue. Most plants that are now on offer under this name are different from Wood's original plant and have really nothing in common with it. A better name for these plants is RUBBISH.

Agapanthus 'Midnight Star'

1989 Raveningham Hall, GB

This dark blue deciduous plant has arching leaves, 40 cm long and 2.6 cm wide. The round peduncle is 50 to 90 cm long, green shaded dark purple at the top. The flat inflorescence, which is 13 to 15 cm in diameter, bears 40 to 50 and sometimes 80 flowers. The glossy flower bud is dark violet blue with a darker base. The flower has a length of 3.5 cm and a diameter of 2.8 cm. The inside is pale violet blue flushed violet and a dark violet blue midrib. The outside is pale violet blue with a distinct purple tinge and a violet blue midrib. The base is glossy violet blue. The stamens are not exserted and the anthers are dark violet. This cultivar is frequently raised from seed. It would, therefore, be preferable to consider this cultivar as a group of plants that resemble each other.

Agapanthus 'Notfred' SILVER MOON

2001 Notcutts Nurseries, GB

Fred Nichols, staff member at Notcutts Nursery, discovered this mutation between seedlings of the so-called Headbourne Hybrids. The name is a combination of Notcutts and Fred Nichols. The trade name is SILVER MOON. The evergreen leaf is 40 cm long and 1.7 cm in diameter, arching and green with cream stripes. The cream-coloured stripes are especially visible at the margin and the young leaves are more yellowish. The base of the leaf is purple. The round peduncle is 70 cm long and pale green with creamy coloured stripes. The flat inflorescence is 19 cm in diameter and bears 40 flowers. The flower bud is violet blue and the flowers are 3.2 cm long and 3.5 cm across. The colour of the flower is violet blue on the inside with a striking purple tinge and a slightly darker midrib. The outside is pale violet blue, also with a striking purple tinge, a darker midrib and violet blue base. The stamens are not exserted and the anthers are black. This plant has received awards both in England and The Netherlands, and a European Plant Variety Right has been applied for. Exceptional about this plant is that it flowers, for many variegated cultivars never flower or only occasionally.

Agapanthus 'Oslo'

2001 Kees Duivenvoorde, Beverwijk, The Netherlands

This pale blue deciduous plant has leaves 40 cm in length and 2.5 cm wide and a more or less round peduncle 100 cm long. The inflorescence is 12 cm in diameter and bears 40 flowers. They are 3.2 cm long and 3.4 cm in diameter. They are pale violet blue both on the inside and outside and have a narrow violet blue midrib. The stamens are exserted and the anthers are violet blue.

Agapanthus 'Peter Pan'

1949 J. N. Giridlian's Oakhurst Gardens, Arcadia, California, USA

The leaves of this blue evergreen are 15 to 25 cm long and 1 cm wide. The round peduncle is 30 to 50 cm long and the flat inflorescence has a diameter of 10 to 12 cm and bears 10 to 15 flowers. The flowers are 3.8 cm long and 4 cm in diameter. They are pale violet blue with a slightly purple tinge and a rather darker midrib. The stamens are not exserted and the anthers are violet. This descrip-

Agapanthus 'Oslo'

Agapanthus 'Peter Pan'

tion could be wrong, however, for hardly anyone knows for certain what the true 'Peter Pan' looks like. According to Dick Fulcher, he has the real plant, but this plant has been propagated by seed on such a large scale that it would be preferable to treat 'Peter Pan' as a group rather than a cultivar. Moreover, the plant is now being micropropagated, so then it is a question of which plants have been used originally. Most plants sold under this name should be considered RUBBISH and have nothing in common with the original plant from Giridlian. It is possible that they never flower.

Agapanthus 'Phantom'

1990 Coleton Fishacre, Devon, GB

'Phantom' was found as a seedling in this garden belonging to the National Trust. The leaves of this very pale blue evergreen are 25 cm in length and 4.5 cm

wide. The green peduncle, which measures 90 to 110 cm in length, has a more or less flat inflorescence of 20 cm and bears 75 flowers. The flowers are 4.5 cm long and 4 cm in diameter. They are white with a pale violet blue blush. The stamens are either not exserted or only partially and the anthers are pale violet with yellow pollen.

Agapanthus 'Pinocchio'

1996 Maas & van Stein, Hillegom, The Netherlands

This blue deciduous plant has pale green foliage which is 30 to 40 cm in length and 1.5 cm across. The round peduncle is 60 cm long and purple at the top. The flat inflorescence is 10 to 13 cm in diameter and bears 30, sometimes 20 or 40 flowers. The violet blue bud has a paler coloured ring above the darker base. The flower is 2.5 cm long and 2.5 cm in diameter. The inside is pale violet blue with a purple blush and a slightly darker

margin, the midrib is violet blue. The outside is violet blue with a darker midrib and a darker base. The stamens are not exserted and the anthers are violet. This plant flowers profusely and is an excellent garden and container plant, but it is not suitable as a cut flower because the stems are too short.

Agapanthus 'Polar Ice'

1981 Maas & van Stein, Hillegom, The Netherlands

This white deciduous plant, which is sometimes compared with 'Glacier Stream', has foliage which is 20 to 30 cm long and 2.5 cm wide. The round peduncles are 60 to 80 cm long. The flat inflorescences have a diameter of 12 to 15 cm and bear 60 to 80 flowers. The white buds are slightly yellowish at the apex. The flowers are 3.2 cm long and 3 cm across. They are white on the inside with a transparent midrib and outside they are white with a very pale yellow

Agapanthus praecox 'Albiflorus'   *Agapanthus* 'Prinses Marilène'

apex. The stamens are not exserted and the anthers are yellow. The greatest difference between this cultivar and 'Glacier Steam' is that the flowers of the latter have a violet tinge and those of 'Polar Ice' are slightly yellow without a trace of violet.

Agapanthus praecox 'Albiflorus'

1864 GB

This *Agapanthus* is an old cultivar which has had plenty of time since 1864 to collect 19 synonyms. This white evergreen has foliage 40 to 70 cm in length and 4.5 cm wide, which is at first upright, later arching. The round, green peduncle is 100 cm long, sometimes 70 or 125 cm. The huge tubular inflorescence of 20 to 25 cm in diameter bears more than 100 flowers. The flower is white both on the inside and the outside and the midrib is transparent. The flower has a slightly purple stem, is 5 cm long and 4.5 cm wide. Everything about this plant is large and awe-inspiring – this being the reason why the plant is still being propagated. The plant has always been propagated from seed, in the past as well as at the present time and, therefore, it would be better to consider this name as the name of a group of plants that resemble each other rather than as a cultivar name.

Agapanthus 'Prinses Marilène'

1998 Kees Duivenvoorde, Beverwijk, The Netherlands

This *Agapanthus* was named after Marilène van den Broek, who married Maurits, Prince of Oranje Nassau in 1998. The pale green arching leaves of this white deciduous plant are 30 cm in length and 2 cm wide. The round peduncle is 70 cm long, pale green and slightly glaucous. The more or less flat inflorescence has a diameter of 15 to 18 cm and bears 15 to 50 flowers. The white flower buds are yellow at the apex and have pale green stems. The flowers are white with a transparent midrib, are 3 cm long and 3.5 cm across. The stamens are exserted and the anthers are cream coloured.

Agapanthus 'Purple Cloud'

1991 New Zealand

This enormously tall, dark blue evergreen is extremely popular. The leaves, which are 50 cm long and 4 cm wide, are impressive. The peduncle is immensely long, from 150 to 200 cm, and is more or less round, green and slightly glaucous. The huge, tubular inflorescence is 20 to 25 cm in diameter and bears 50 to 70 flowers. The flowers are 4.5 cm long and 3 to 3.5 cm across. The inside is pale to normal violet blue with a paler base and a dark violet blue midrib and margin. The outside is dark violet blue with a purple base. The first flowers are pendulous, a fact that gives away their *inapertus* origins, but the other flowers are more or less horizontal. The fruits are of interest, too, for they are green and on the sun side violet at the base and along the ribs. Because these plants produce hardly any side shoots they are difficult to increase vegatatively. They used to be propagated by seed but today this is carried out on a large scale by micropropagation. Plants that are propagated from seed can be smaller and less impressive than the true cultivar.

Agapanthus 'Queen Mother'

1995 The Crown Estate, Windsor, GB

This *Agapanthus* is named after Lady Elizabeth Bowes-Lyon (1900–2002), Her Majesty Queen Elizabeth, the beloved mother of the present queen of England, Her Majesty Queen Elizabeth II. This is the reason why this plant sells in England; otherwise it is just an ordinary blue *Agapanthus*. The leaves of this blue deciduous plant are 50 cm in length and 2.5 cm wide. The round peduncle is 60 to 85 cm in length and has a flat inflorescence with a diameter of 12 to 15 cm. It bears 30 to 40, sometimes 80 flowers. The flowers which emerge from the dark violet flower bud are 2.7 to 3 cm long and 2.5 to 3 cm in diameter. The inside is violet blue with a lighter base, a darker midrib and a slightly purple margin. The outside is violet blue with a slightly darker midrib and base. The stamens are not exserted and the anthers are violet blue.

Agapanthus 'Rosemary'

1974 Lewis Palmer, GB

This pale blue (grey) deciduous plant has leaves that are 50, sometimes 70 cm long and 3.5 cm wide. The sturdy, round peduncle is 100 to 140 cm long and has a more or less flat inflorescence, diameter 15 to 19 cm, and bears 50 to 70 flowers.

Agapanthus 'Purple Cloud'

Agapanthus 'Queen Mother'

Agapanthus 'Rosemary'

Agapanthus 'San Gabriel' flower

Agapanthus 'San Gabriel' foliage

Agapanthus 'Septemberhemel'

The flower buds are greenish white and slightly flushed with violet. The flowers are 3.7 to 4 cm in length and 2.5 cm in diameter. The inside is white to very pale purplish grey, with a transparent, slightly purple tinged midrib. The outside is white at the margin to very pale greyish violet, with a greenish base and a transparent midrib. The stamens are not exserted and the anthers are black. Because of its unusual grey colour, this plant is very easy to combine with flowers that are much harsher in colour.

Agapanthus 'San Gabriel'

1986 Monrovia Nursery Company, Azusa, California, USA

This variegated plant was discovered in a bed of seedlings and named after the hills in the neighbourhood of the nursery. It is a blue evergreen with arching leaves that are 30 cm in length and 2.2 cm wide. There are differently coloured

leaves on each plant. This varies from a few glossy plain green leaves to a few that are pale to dark yellow striped, and some of the leaves are even plain yellow with a green base. The round peduncle, which is 60 to 75 cm long, is green with cream-coloured stripes. The flat inflorescence has a diameter of 15 cm and carries 40 flowers. The flowers are 4 cm long and wide and the inside is very pale violet blue to almost white with a pale violet blue margin that is flushed purple. The midrib is pale violet blue. The outside of the flower is violet blue with a darker coloured midrib and a slightly darker base. In one and the same inflorescence the colour of the fruits can vary from yellow and green to striped. 'San Gabriel' is a good variegated plant that also flowers, providing it is propagated vegetatively and not from seed. A problem can be that it does not always remain variegated. Green shoots should, therefore, be removed.

Agapanthus 'Septemberhemel'

2000 Hans Kramer, De Hessenhof, Ede, The Netherlands

The name of this blue deciduous *Agapanthus* is very appropriate for it is a late flowerer. Hans Kramer selected this plant from a bed of 2000 seedlings. The leaves are 35 cm in length and 2.3 cm wide. The sturdy, round peduncle is 70 cm long and has a flat inflorescence 14 cm in diameter, with 60 to 70 flowers. The flower bud is dark purple, just as its stem. The slightly pendulous flower is 3.6 cm long and 3.4 cm across. The inside is pale violet blue with just a touch of purple at the apex and a dark violet blue margin. The midrib is violet blue. The outside of the plant is violet blue with a purple tinge, and the midrib is slightly darker with a dark violet blue base. The stamens are not exserted and the anthers are violet at first and change to black later. 'Septemberhemel' is a

cross between 'Lilliput' and 'Midnight Star'. 'Septemberhemel' resembles 'Loch Hope' but the peduncle is sturdier and straight.

Agapanthus 'Silver Mist'

1993 Dick Fulcher, Bicton College, Devon, GB

The leaves of this pale blue evergreen are 20 to 65 cm long and 4 cm wide. The flat peduncle is 75 to 95 cm long and has a tubular inflorescence 20 cm in diameter, which bears 70 flowers. They are very pale violet blue, 3 to 3.4 cm long and 3.7 cm in diameter. The stamens are either not exserted or just a little and the anther is purple.

Agapanthus 'Sky Rocket'

1993 Dick Fulcher, Bicton College, GB

This blue deciduous plant came originally from the *Agapanthus* collection at Bicton College and was selected by Dick Fulcher. The leaf length varies from 20 to 65 cm and it is 2.5 to 3 cm wide. The exceptionally sturdy peduncle is 100 to 140, sometimes 175 cm, in length and is somewhat flat. The pendulous inflorescence has a diameter of 14 cm and bears 70 drooping flowers. The flower bud, which is erect at first but later drooping, is pale violet blue with some green at the centre. The flower is 4.8 to 5 cm long and 2.3 to 2.4 cm in diameter. The inside is very pale violet blue with a slightly deeper purple margin and a violet blue to purple midrib. The outside is purple flushed violet blue and the midrib is slightly darker. The stamens are not exserted, although sometimes one or two protrude a little,

and the anthers are violet at first and black later.

Agapanthus 'Stéphanie'

2000 Ignace van Doorslaer, Melle-Gontrode, Belgium

This evergreen white *Agapanthus* is named after a student who was working at Ignace van Doorslaer's nursery. The tubular inflorescence has a diameter of 13 to 15 cm and bears an unbelievable number of flowers, 80 to 100. The peduncles are 80 cm long. The flower bud is greenish white and has a green stem. The flowers are white both on the inside and outside and the midrib is slightly darker. When they are out of flower they are still white. The stamens are exserted and the anthers are black.

Agapanthus 'Stéphanie Charm'

Agapanthus 'Streamline'

Agapanthus 'Sunfield'

Agapanthus 'Stéphanie Charm'

1999 Ignace van Doorslaer, Melle-Gontrode, Belgium

This white deciduous plant, a seedling from 'Stéphanie', has 40-cm-long and 2.5-cm-wide leaves. The round peduncle is 40 to 60 cm long and has a tubular inflorescence 11 to 13 cm in diameter. This inflorescence can bear 40 to 100 flowers. They are 3.5 cm long and 4 cm in diameter and are white with a transparent midrib. The buds are white with a touch of yellow whilst 'Stéphanie' has buds that are white with a touch of green.

Agapanthus 'Streamline'

1991 Auckland Botanical Garden, New Zealand

The more or less evergreen foliage is 20 cm in length and each leaf is 1.2 cm in diameter. The flat peduncle is 50 cm long and has an inflorescence of 10 to 13 cm, bearing 15 to 25 flowers. The flowers which are 4 cm long and 3.5 to 4 cm in diameter are very pale violet blue. The stamens are not exserted and the anthers are violet blue. Because this plant has been greatly propagated by sowing and shows great variation it has not got a good name. As the plant is now being propagated by micropropagation it is hoped that it will retrieve its good reputation.

Agapanthus 'Sunfield'

1987 Gebr. J. P. & N. M. Zonneveld, Heemskerk, The Netherlands

This plant was given to the Zonneveld brothers as an unnamed seedling. It was given its name by the person who introduced it but then translated into English. The foliage of this blue deciduous plant is 50 to 60 cm in length and 4.5 cm wide; the width of the leaf proves that the theory that plants with wide leaves are evergreen is not correct. The more or less flat, sturdy peduncle is 100 cm long and has a large, tubular inflorescence with diameter of 23 cm. It bears 50 to 80 flowers. The flower buds are dark violet blue and the stem is green with purple marks. The flower is pale violet blue on the inside, even paler at the base, the midrib is darker and the margin is flushed purple. The outside is violet blue with purple and the midrib is deeper purple at the apex and even darker at the base. The flowers are 3.5 cm long and 3.5 cm in diameter. The stamens are not exserted and the anthers are dark violet.

Agapanthus 'Sylvine'

1997 Ignace van Doorslaer, Melle-Gontrode, Belgium

Sylvine is Ignace van Doorslaer's daughter; he named this blue deciduous plant after her. The leaves are 40 cm long and 2.5 cm wide; the round, green peduncle is 70 cm long. The tubular inflorescence, which has a diameter of 16 cm, bears 60 to 70 flowers. The flower buds are dark violet blue and have green stems, tinged purple. The flower, which is 3.2 to 3.4 cm long and 3.5 cm wide, is violet blue on the inside with a slightly paler margin and a violet blue midrib. On the outside the flower is violet blue with a purple tinge and the midrib is dark violet blue with a purple apex. The stamens are not exserted and the anther is violet. 'Sylvine' is a wonderful, late-flowering, dark blue cultivar.

Agapanthus 'Timaru'

2001 New Zealand

A popular plant that was named after a province of New Zealand. The plant is evergreen; it has a peduncle measuring 75 cm in length and it bears violet blue flowers.

Agapanthus 'Tinkerbell'

1991 New Zealand

This is a variegated *Agapanthus* that hardly ever flowers. The label on the plant often shows a flowering plant, but the photographer has probably inserted a few flowers in between the variegated leaves. The name of the pixie in the fairy tale *Peter Pan* is applicable because this cultivar is a sport of 'Peter Pan' but, considering that 'Peter Pan' is propagated by seed throughout the world, it is probably more likely that 'Tinkerbell' is a mutant rather than a sport. The leaf of this evergreen variegated *Agapanthus* is 30 cm long and 1 cm wide. It is, therefore, narrower than that of the variegated 'San Gabriel'. Moreover, the plant is recognisable because the foliage lies flat on the ground. It is pale green with thin, yellow stripes and a wide, yellow margin. It is cream coloured at the base.

Although 'Tinkerbell' has the reputation of being difficult to propagate, this is not apparent. After two years you will have quite a pot full of them.

Agapanthus 'Umbellatus Albus'

1888 probably The Netherlands

This plant has been propagated from seed for such a long time that it would be better to speak of a group of plants that are more or less the same than of a cultivar. It is a white deciduous plant with foliage that is 20 to 50 cm long and 1.5 to 2.5 cm wide. The round peduncle is 80 to 100 cm long. The more or less tubular inflorescence has a diameter of 15 cm and the number of flowers varies from 30 to 50 (sometimes 20, but sometimes also 80). This plant often shows a "pagoda" shaped fasciation. The flower bud is greenish white with purple at the apex and has a purple flower stem. The

Agapanthus 'Sylvine'

Agapanthus 'Tinkerbell'

Agapanthus 'Umbellatus Albus'

Agapanthus 'Virginia'

Agapanthus 'Volendam'

Agapanthus 'Waga'

flower is 2.3 to 3.3 cm long and 3 cm in diameter. The inside is white with a transparent midrib and the outside is white with a midrib that is pale purple at the apex. This plant often flowers twice. Plants on offer under the name *Agapanthus africanus* generally belong to this cultivar. It is just an "ordinary" *Agapanthus* that has been in propagation for more than 100 years.

Agapanthus 'Virginia'

2000 Kees Duivenvoorde, Beverwijk, The Netherlands

This plant is named after the state of Virginia in the USA. This white evergreen has leaves that are 30 to 40 cm long and 3 to 4 cm wide. The flat, green peduncle is 40 to 60 cm long, sometimes 80 cm, and has a more or less flat inflorescence which is 16 to 18 cm in diameter and bears 40 to 60, sometimes 80, flowers. The white flower bud has a pale green stem. The large flower, which is

4.5 to 4.7 cm long and 5 cm in diameter, is white on the inside with a white, not transparent, hardly visible midrib. The outside is also white, at the base too. When they have finished flowering they usually drop off. The stamens are exserted and the anthers are yellow. There is usually no fruit. 'Virginia' is too short-stemmed for a cut flower but is excellent as a pot plant.

Agapanthus 'Volendam'

2001 Kees Duivenvoorde, Beverwijk, The Netherlands

One of the most purely white cultivars, this plant was named after a famous tourist village in The Netherlands. The foliage of this white deciduous plant is green and upright. The peduncle is 80 cm long and the flat inflorescence is 15 cm in diameter and bears 30 to 40 flowers. They are white, both on the inside and outside. The stamens are exserted and the anthers provide an extra white

effect for they are yellow. 'Volendam' is an excellent cut flower.

Agapanthus 'Waga'

2001 Th. P. W. de Groot, Hillegom, The Netherlands

This cultivar was introduced by Maas & van Stein and was named after the River Vaga (in Dutch, Waga). The leaves of this blue deciduous plant are 45 cm long and 3.3 cm wide. The flat peduncle is 80 cm long and has a flat inflorescence of 15 to 22 cm which bears 40 flowers. The flower, which is 3.8 to 4 cm long and 3.6 to 4 cm in diameter, has 8 to 12 tepals. The flower is very pale violet blue on the inside with a violet blue midrib. The outside is also very pale violet blue but has a slightly darker midrib. The outside is purple flushed green. The stamens are not exserted and the anthers are greenish brown.

Agapanthus 'White Beauty'

1970, 2001 Reintjes, Veulen, The Netherlands

The cut flower grower Reintjes selected this plant in 1970 from a number of plants that he received as being white flowering and named it 'White Superior'. In 2001 he renamed the plant 'White Beauty', according to the rules. The leaves of this white deciduous plant are 40 cm long and 2.5 cm wide. The more or less flat peduncle is 70 to 90 cm long and has a flat inflorescence 18 cm in diameter, which bears 60 to 80 flowers. The greenish white flower bud, which is slightly purple at the top, has a purple green stem. The flower is 4.3 cm long and 3.5 to 3.8 cm in diameter. The inside is white with a narrow midrib that is more or less transparent. The three outer tepals are purple or violet purple on the outside and the three inner tepals sometimes have a violet purple midrib. The stamens are not exserted and the anthers are first purple and later black.

Agapanthus 'White Heaven'

C. J. de Jong & A. Ph. M. Rijnbeek and Son Ltd., Boskoop, The Netherlands

An impressive white evergreen which has leaves that are 60 cm long and 3.5 to 5 cm wide. The flat peduncle, which is 70 to 80 cm long, has an enormous tubular inflorescence 20 to 24 cm in diameter, bearing 50 to 80 flowers. The flower bud is white and pale greenish white at the base and has a green stem. The flower is 4.5 to 5 cm long and 5 cm in diameter and generally consists of 8 to 10 lobes. The flower is white on the inside with a slightly transparent midrib and on the outside it is white with a slightly darker white base. When out of flower they are white. The flowers are horizontal to slightly nodding but there are a number of upright flowers in every inflorescence. There are usually a number of fasciations within an inflorescence. Only one or two stamens are exserted and the anthers are yellow. The fruits are green. This plant has European Plant Variety Right and at the Plantarium 2003 was awarded a silver medal.

Agapanthus 'White Smile'

1996 Maas & van Stein, Hillegom, The Netherlands

This plant was propagated far earlier than 1996 under the name *laag wit* ("low white") and was only renamed 'White Smile' in 1996. The leaves of this white deciduous plant are 40 to 50 cm in length and up to 2.5 cm in width. The flat peduncle is 80 cm long and has a flat inflorescence, which is 16 cm in diameter and consists of 40 to 50 flowers. The cream-coloured flower buds with a pale purple apex are upright at first but soon begin to nod. The flower is 3.7 cm long

and 4 to 4.5 cm in diameter. The inside is white with a narrow, transparent midrib and the outside is white with pale purple on the tepals that are facing the sun. The stamens are slightly exserted and the anthers are violet yellow. The fruits are green with a purple flush.

Agapanthus 'White Superior'

1997 Bristol Botanical Gardens, GB

This white deciduous *Agapanthus* has 80 to 140 cm long peduncles. The more or less flat inflorescences bear 40 to 60 flowers. The upright cream-coloured flower bud has a purple apex and the flower itself is white, both on the inside and the outside. The stamens are exserted and the anthers are orange brown.

Agapanthus 'Whitney'

1999 C. H. A. van Eijk, Nootdorp, The Netherlands

This plant, which is named after a place in South Africa, has been awarded Kwekersrecht (plant variety right) in The Netherlands. The leaf of this white evergreen is 30 to 35 cm long and 1.5 to 1.7 cm wide. The round peduncle is 40 to 50 cm long and has a flat inflorescence with a diameter of 15 cm. Although there are only 20 to 30 flowers in an inflorescence, the plant flowers profusely and easily and is, therefore, popular as a pot plant. The white flower bud has a yellowish green apex and a green stem. The flowers are 4.2 cm long and 4.5 cm in diameter. On the inside they are white with a transparent midrib and on the outside they are also white. They are also white when out of flower. The stamens are slightly exserted and the anthers are yellow. This plant's flowering period is often brought forward so that it is on sale at the florist's in April and May, in flower. This is not a positive development because the purchasers are unable to get the plant to flower the following year, and, in this way, *Agapanthus* can become degraded to being a disposable plant.

Agapanthus 'Windlebrooke'

1995 The Crown Estate, Windsor, GB

The leaves of this dark blue deciduous plant are 15 cm long and 1.4 cm wide. The round peduncle is 30 to 40 cm long and has an inflorescence that is 8 to 9 cm in diameter and bears 20 to 30 flowers. The flower bud is dark violet blue. The flower is 2.5 cm long and 3 cm across. The inside is dark violet blue with a slightly darker midrib and a purple tinged margin. The outside is violet blue.

Agapanthus 'Windsor Grey'

1995 The Crown Estate, Windsor, GB

The leaves of this light blue, almost grey *Agapanthus* are 70 cm long and 4 cm wide. The peduncle is 100 to 130 cm tall and has an inflorescence of 19 to 22 cm. This inflorescence varies from flat to round, the more flowers the rounder, and the number of flowers varies from 70 to 100. The flower is 4.2 cm long and 2.6 cm across and is very pale violet blue with a transparent midrib. The base is greenish because the ovary shines through. The flowers of 'Windsor Grey' are practically identical to those of 'Rosemary', but those of 'Windsor Grey' are slightly darker. Both have an unusual, almost grey colour.

RUBBISH

In the middle of the nineteenth century the word RUBBISH was used in the bulb trade for bulbs, corms, tubers and plants, like *Agapanthus*, which were traded as dry products. Those plants that were not sold were made up into small parcels and sold under the name RUBBISH. Anything could be in these small parcels; it was certainly not rubbish but more likely to be surplus stock composed of various plants. Nowadays, it is not possible to buy such surplus batches of plants because the trade requires plants to be named and, moreover, the customer is not keen on such surprise packages.

However, Wim Snoeijer has reintroduced the name RUBBISH for *Agapanthus* because so many of these plants are propagated from seed, and plants thus propagated do not possess exactly the same qualities as the parent plant. These plants are then sold, without mentioning whether they have been propagated from seed or from some other source. Some of these sown plants are even sold without ever having flowered. These plants are then often sold under the name Headbourne Hybrids. Sometimes plants are sold in one land under a certain cultivar name, whilst in a different land the same name is used for a plant with different qualities. If both these plants have been propagated vegetatively then one of them should be given another name.
There are still cultivars that have been propagated from seed which do not really deserve a cultivar name. These are plants that should be grouped with

plants they resemble instead of being designated cultivars. Only those plants that have been propagated vegetatively have a right to be called a cultivar. Even worse is a situation where *Agapanthus* plants which have been propagated by seed are used for micropropagation.

It must be presumed that plants that are bred by micropropagation are vegetatively propagated plants, otherwise more and more plants will be coming onto the market on a large scale which should be designated RUBBISH instead of having a cultivar name. Both the breeder and the customer can see to it that these practices are stopped. The breeder, by propagating vegetatively, and the customer, by only buying named plants and by not being taken in by RUBBISH, such as the *Agapanthus* Headbourne Hybrids, *Agapanthus* blue, and *Agapanthus* white.

The ICNCP-1995 accepts cultivars propagated from seed. Most vegetables and annual flowers are sold as seed. But *Agapanthus* plants that have been propagated from seed show great variety, even though that seed has been collected from a plant that is growing on its own. That is why it is unacceptable that these plants are propagated from seed. It is a pity because *Agapanthus* is very easy to propagate from seed.
There are so many advantages to buying a named plant that has been propagated vegetatively that it is very well worth

while going in search of one. At a good nursery the customer has the choice between evergreen and deciduous, tall or low plants, with many or few flowers. It is about time that people realise that *Agapanthus* is a plant just like every other properly named garden or container plant.

Lists

Bunches of *Agapanthus* at a market in Portugal

Lists make our lives easier. Having an overall picture can help create order out of chaos. Make a quick choice and then have a further look to see if it really is the right choice. Doing this beforehand is preferable to just picking something up at a garden show or at a nursery. Back home, it can then prove to be an evergreen *Agapanthus* whilst it should have been a border plant. Always choose a plant when it is in flower and check that it is what it should be. With the right treatment an *Agapanthus* can last a lifetime, so making a choice involves more than just deciding, on the spur of the moment, between a white or a blue plant.

Deciduous or evergreen, and flower colour

The choice between deciduous and evergreen is important and has to do with the way in which a plant survives the winter. Whoever opts for an evergreen knows that it must be treated as a container plant. In winter it must be kept indoors in a light, frost-free and cool place (not warmer than 8C). A deciduous plant can, under the right circumstances, remain in the ground outside, provided it receives the necessary care and a winter cover. A deciduous plant can also be treated like a container plant. The place where it is to spend the winter must meet with same temperature requirements as an evergreen but a deciduous plant may be kept in the dark.

Agapanthus 'Lady Grey'
Deciduous and pale blue

Agapanthus 'Amsterdam'
Deciduous and dark blue

There are only two *Agapanthus* colours, blue and white. Nevertheless, there are enormous varieties within the range of these two colours. In order to make the choice easier, here follows a list of pale blue, blue, dark blue and white. Of course, there is no uniform colour to be found in these groups. Sometimes a pale blue colour tends to be closer to grey, sometimes closer to purple. Dark blue varies also, and the list with blue flowers shows the most gradations between pale blue and dark blue. There are even different shades of white, which is not really a colour. Two groups of white *Agapanthus* can be distinguished. One group is white with a touch of blue or purple, the other group is pure white or has a touch of yellow or green. A detailed colour description can be found in the extensive descriptions of the cultivars.

To enable a quick choice to be made, the flower colour and whether a plant is evergreen or deciduous have been combined.

Deciduous and pale blue
'Castle of Mey'
'Lady Grey'
'Liam's Lilac'
'Mariètte'
'Oslo'
'Rosemary'
'Sky Rocket'
'Waga'

Deciduous and blue
'Blue Heaven'
'Blue Triumphator'
'Blue Velvet'
'Catharina'
'Cobalt Blue'
'Donau'
'Dr Brouwer'
'Elisabeth'
'Marianne'
'Pinocchio'
'Queen Mother'
'Septemberhemel'

Deciduous and dark blue
'Amsterdam'
'Black Beauty'
'Bressingham Blue'
'Bristol'
'Columba'
'Copenhagen'
'Graskop'
'Graskopje'
'Intermedius'
'Isis'
'Lilliput'
'Loch Hope'
'Midnight Blue'
'Midnight Star'
'Sunfield'
'Sylvine'
'Windlebrooke'

Deciduous and white (touch of purple)
'Ardernei'
'Bressingham White'
'Franni'
'Glacier Stream'
'Lady Moore'
'Leicester'
'Umbellatus Albus'
'White Beauty'
'White Smile'
'White Superior'

Deciduous and white (pure white, touch of green or yellow)
'Duivenbrugge White'
'Ice Lolly'
'Polar Ice'
'Prinses Marilène'
'Stéphanie Charm'
'Volendam'

Agapanthus 'Ardernei'
Deciduous and white

Agapanthus 'Blue Giant'
Evergreen and pale blue

Agapanthus 'Stéphanie Charm'
Evergreen and white

Evergreen and pale blue
'Angela'
'Blue Giant'
'Blue Moon'
'Ellamae'
'Gayle's Lilac'
'Lilac Time'
'Phantom'
'Silver Mist'
'Streamline'
'Windsor Grey'

Evergreen and blue
'Blue Globe'
'Flore Pleno'
'Glen Avon'
'Jack's Blue'
'Jodie'
'Peter Pan'
'Timaru'

Evergreen and dark blue
'Purple Cloud'

Evergreen and white (touch of purple)
A. praecox 'Albiflorus'

Evergreen and white (pure white, touch of green or yellow)
'Stéphanie'
'Virginia'
'White Heaven'
'Whitney'

From XS to XL
There is quite some variety in the height of *Agapanthus* plants. The height is that of the peduncle, which always rises above the foliage. 'Lilliput', which with a height of 20 to 60 cm lives up to its name, is a dwarf when compared to the gigantic 'Purple Cloud', which can reach a height of 150 to 200 cm. The inflorescence is usually related to the height of the plant. 'Lilliput' has an inflorescence which is 10 cm in diameter and bears 20 to 25 flowers whereas the diameter of the 'Purple Cloud' inflorescence is 20 to 25 cm and bears 50 to 70 flowers.

Extra small/dwarf (up to 50 cm)
'Gayle's Lilac'
'Lilliput'
'Midnight Blue'
'Peter Pan'
'White Smile'
'Whitney'
'Windlebrooke'

Small/low (50 to 70 cm)
'Amsterdam'
'Black Beauty'
'Castle of Mey'
'Columba'
'Donau'
'Intermedius'
'Lady Grey'
'Lady Moore'
'Leicester'
'Marianne'
'Mariètte'
'Pinocchio'
'Polar Ice'
'Stéphanie Charm'
'Streamline'
'Virginia'

Agapanthus 'Lilliput'
Extra small

Agapanthus 'Donau'
Small

Agapanthus 'Catharina'
Medium

Medium/middle (70 to 90 cm)
'Ardernei'
'Blue Heaven'
'Blue Moon'
'Blue Triumphator'
'Bressingham Blue'
'Bressingham White'
'Bristol'
'Catharina'
'Dr Brouwer'
'Duivenbrugge White'
'Elisabeth'
'Flore Pleno'
'Franni'
'Ice Lolly'
'Isis'
'Liam's Lilac'
'Midnight Star'
'Phantom'
'Prinses Marilène'
'Queen Mother'
'Septemberhemel'
'Silver Mist'
'Stéphanie'
'Sylvine'
'Timaru'

'Umbellatus Albus'
'Volendam'
'Waga'
'White Beauty'
'White Heaven'

Large/tall (100 to 120 cm)
'Albatross'
'Angela'
'Blue Globe'
'Blue Velvet'
'Cobalt Blue'
'Copenhagen'
'Ellamae'
'Glacier Stream'
'Glen Avon'
'Graskop'
'Jack's Blue'
'Lilac Time'
'Loch Hope'
'Oslo'
A. praecox 'Albiflorus'
'Rosemary'
'Sunfield'
'Windsor Grey'

Extra large (120 cm and taller)
'Blue Giant'
'Jodie'
'Purple Cloud'
'Sky Rocket'
'White Superior'

Flat, round or nodding inflorescence
The individual flowers of an *Agapanthus* are grouped together in an umbel at the top of a round or flat peduncle. The shape of the umbel can vary from flat to round and all the gradations in between, from more or less flat to more or less round. Then there are also nodding, or drooping, umbels, in which the flowers in bud are upright but, when open, all droop. The size of the flower umbel varies from a diameter of 10 cm, as in 'Peter Pan' and 'Pinocchio', to 25 cm in 'Purple Cloud'. The number of flowers in each inflorescence varies enormously from 10 to 15 in 'Peter Pan' to 100 to 150 in 'Ellamae'; 'Glen Avon' even has 350 flowers. The size and shape of the individual flowers vary, and an inflores-

Agapanthus 'Glacier Stream'
Flat inflorescence

Agapanthus 'Dr Brouwer'
Round inflorescence

Agapanthus 'Sky Rocket'
Nodding inflorescence

cence is the sum of all these factors. Only the difference in umbel has been listed. Perhaps some people prefer a round inflorescence, in which the flowers are in the shape of a globe which is perched at the top of the peduncle. Others will prefer a flat inflorescence with a flattened half globe.

Flat inflorescence
'Blue Moon'
'Bressingham Blue'
'Bressingham White'
'Castle of Mey' (more or less)
'Donau'
'Glacier Stream'
'Intermedius'
'Isis'
'Lady Moore'
'Leicester'
'Lilliput'
'Loch Hope'
'Midnight'
'Peter Pan'
'Phantom' (more or less)
'Pinocchio'

'Polar Ice'
'Prinses Marilène'
'Queen Mother'
'Rosemary' (more or less)
'Septemberhemel'
'Virginia' (more or less)
'Volendam'
'Waga'
'White Beauty'
'White Smile'
'White Superior' (more or less)
'Whitney'
'Windsor Grey' (from flat to tubular)

Round inflorescence
'Albatross' (more or less)
'Amsterdam'
'Angela' (more or less)
'Ardernei' (more or less)
'Black Beauty'
'Blue Giant'
'Blue Globe'
'Blue Heaven'
'Blue Triumphator'
'Blue Velvet'
'Bristol'

'Catharina'
'Cobalt Blue' (more or less)
'Columba'
'Copenhagen'
'Dr Brouwer'
'Duivenbrugge White'
'Elisabeth'
'Ellamae'
'Glen Avon'
'Ice Lolly'
'Lady Grey'
'Lilac Time'
'Marianne'
'Mariëtte'
'Oslo'
A. praecox 'Albiflorus'
'Purple Cloud'
'Silver Mist'
'Stéphanie'
'Stéphanie Charm'
'Sunfield'
'Sylvine'
'Umbellatus Albus' (more or less)
'White Heaven'

Agapanthus 'San Gabriel'
Variegated leaves

Nodding inflorescence
'Graskop'
'Sky Rocket'

Variegated leaves
Variegated plants are always a freak of nature. There are many plants with variegated leaves and *Agapanthus* is no exception; it has a few variegated cultivars. The flowers of these variegated plants do not play such an important role, and sometimes it would be preferable if they did not appear at all for they add little to the plant's attraction. Variegated is colourful enough. Most of the variegated cultivars are evergreen.

'Argenteus Vittatus'
'Aureovittatus'
'Beth Chatto'
'Goldfinger'
'Hinag' SUMMER GOLD
'Meibont' (only variegated in May)
'Notfred' SILVER MOON
'San Gabriel'
'Tinkerbell'

Fragrance

Agapanthus used to be called a hyacinth, but this could never be correct, even if one just considers the fragrance, or lack of it. You are never tempted to stick your nose into an *Agapanthus* flower because the flowers are not scented. Or are they? Some time ago two cultivars came onto the market that had, apparently, a very strong scent; the white 'Fragrant Snow' and the blue 'Fragrant Glen'. Articles were written about these plants with their glorious scent. However, these cultivars have disappeared from the market and are nowhere to be found. This is no wonder for their names have been changed. 'Fragrant Snow' is now 'Snow Cloud' and 'Fragrant Glen' is 'Glen Avon'. There was even a third fragrant cultivar 'Fragrant Blue' and this flower is now named 'Blue Brush'. Just as 'Glen Avon' and 'Snow Cloud', 'Blue Brush' hails from New Zealand. Perhaps the names have been changed because the flowers were not as fragrant as was at first thought. Although *Agapanthus* is not one of the most scented of flowers it does spread some fragrance, especially when there are many flowering plants in a small space indoors.

Literature

Dr. C. A. **Backer** (2000). *Verklarend woordenboek van wetenschappelijke plantennamen* (Explanatory Dictionary of Scientific Plant Names). Publisher: L. J. Veen, Amsterdam/Antwerp.

S. **Bleeker** (1927). *Geïllustreerd Handboek over Bloemisterij* (Illustrated Manual of Florists).

Hanneke van **Dijk** (2002). 'De Nederlandse Planten Collectie van *Agapanthus*.' In: *Tuin & Landschap* 19. 'The Dutch Plant Collection of *Agapanthus*'.

Hanneke van **Dijk** & Mineke **Kurpershoek** (2002). *Bloembollenencyclopedie* (Encyclopaedia of Bulbs). Rebo International, Lisse.

Hanneke van **Dijk** & Wim **Snoeijer** (2001). *Nederlandse Planten Collecties* (Dutch Plant Collections). Tuinenreisgids Gottmer, Haarlem. (Garden Guides).

Graham Duncan (1998). *Grow Agapanthus*. Kirstenbosch Gardening Series, National Botanical Institute, Kirstenbosch.

Dick **Fulcher** (2000). 'From Africa with love.' In: *The Garden*, Journal of the Royal Horticultural Society, Augustus, pages 592–597.

Dick **Fulcher** (2002). *Agapanthus and other plants*. Pine Cottage Plants, Fourways, Devon, GB.

A. J. M. **Gillissen** (1980). *Sortimentsonderzoek van het geslacht* Agapanthus (Research into the varieties of the *Agapanthus* genus).

Frances M. **Leighton** (1965). 'The Genus *Agapanthus* L'Héritier.' In: Journal of South African Botany, Suppl. Vol. No. IV.

Marianne **North** (1980) *A vision of Eden, the life and work of Marianne North*. Royal Botanic Gardens, Kew, and Webb & Bower, Exeter.

Chris **Philip** & Tony **Lord**. *RHS Plant Finder 2003–2004*. Dorling Kindersley, London.

Kristo **Pienaar** (1987). *A-Z of Garden Flowers in South Africa*. C. Struik Publishers, Cape Town.

W. **Robinson** (1897) 5th edition. *The English Flower Garden*. John Murray, London.

Wim **Snoeijer** (1995). '*Agapanthus*.' In: *De Parel*, bericht van de Oranjerievereniging (article from The Orangery Society).

Wim **Snoeijer** (1998). *Agapanthus: A Review*. Wim Snoeijer, Gouda.

Wim **Snoeijer** (2004). *Agapanthus: A Revision of the Genus*. Timber Press, Portland, USA.

Rick **Wortelboer** (2003). *Plantenvinder voor de lage landen* (Plant Finder for the Low Countries). Terra/Lannoo, Warnsveld.

B. J. M. **Zonneveld** & G. D. **Duncan** (2003). Taxonomic implications of genome size and pollen color and vitality for species of *Agapanthus* L'Héritier (Agapanthaceae). In Plant Syst. Ev.

Addresses

The Netherlands

Kwekerij De Border
Twickelerlaan 13
7495 VG Ambt-Delden
Tel. 074-3764123
www.border.nl
1 March – 1 December, every
afternoon from 13.00 to
17.00, Saturdays from 9.00 to
17.00, closed on Sundays and
national holidays.

Collectie Kees Duivenvoorde
Alkmaarseweg 125
1947 DC Beverwijk
Tel. 0251-224184
Collection of more than 200
Agapanthus cultivars. No
sales, visits by appointment.

Engelse Landschapstuin d'n Nooteboom
Oud Zevenaarsedijk 4
Zevenaar
Tel. 0316-248105 or 248106
15 May – 15 September on
Sundays from 10.00 to 17.00.
Group visits by appointment.

Tuingoed Foltz
Hereweg 3346
9651 AT Meeden (Gr.)
Tel. 0598-635000
Fax 0598-653750
www.tuingoedfoltz.nl
Mid March to Christmas,
Tuesday to Saturday, from
10.00 to 17.00 and the first
and third Sunday of the
month from 11.00 to 17.00.

Kwekerij De Hessenhof
Hans Kramer
Hessenweg 41
6718 TC Ede
Tel. 0318-617334
Fax 0318-612773
www.hessenhof.nl
1 March to 15 November,
Thursday, Friday and
Saturday from 9.00 to 17.00.

Coen Jansen Vaste Planten
Ankummer Es 13a
7722 RD Dalfsen
Tel. 0529-434086
Fax 0529-436889
coenjansenvasteplanten@hot-
mail.com
March to mid November,
Wednesday, Thursday, Friday
and Saturday from 10.00 to
17.00. June, July and August
also on Tuesday.

G. Lacor
Zandweg 3
4416 NA Kruiningen
Tel. 0113-381133
Visit by telephone appoint-
ment only.

Kwekerij De Morgen
Dick de Winter
Obdammerdijk 21
1713 RA Obdam
Tel. 06-25046056
Fax 0226-450883
www.newgenerationplants.nl
March to January, Tuesday to
Saturday from 10.00 to 17.00.

NPC *Agapanthus*,
Dutch cultivars
Kasteel Rosendael
Rosendael 1
6891 DA Rozendaal
Contact person: Gerard
Achterstraat
Tel. 026-361 3922, 06-1350
4019
Fax 026-361 3922
www.kasteelrosendael.nl
Park Rosendael, 1 May to 31
October, Tuesday to
Saturday from 10.00 to 17.00,
Sundays from 11.00 to 17.00.

Dutch *Agapanthus* Dagen
Huis Verwolde
Jonker Emilelaan 4
7245 TL Laren (gemeente
Lochem)
Contact person: Gerrit
Pleijter
Tel. 0573-40 18 25
In July (varying dates)

Belgium

Ignace van Doorslaer
Kapellendries 52
B9090 Melle-Gontrode
Tel. 0032-9-252 11 23
Fax 0032-9-252 44 55
Order via internet:
www.Agapanthus-
Internationaal.com
By telephone appointment
only.

Arboretum Kalmthout
Heuvel 2
2920 Kalmthout
Tel. 0032-3-666 67 41

Koen van Poucke
Heistraat 106
B-9100 Sint-Niklaas
Tel. 0032-3-7777642
Fax 0032-3-7661698
www.koenvanpoucke.be
Tuesday to Saturday from 9
to 12.30 and from 13.00 to
18.00. Sundays from 9.30 to
12.30. Mondays closed.
Closed in July.

Great Britain

Apple Court
Hordle Lane
Lymington
Hampshire SO41 0HU
www.applecourt.com

Ballyrogan Gardens
Gary Dunlop
Ballyrogan
Newtownards Down
Northern Ireland BT23 4SD

Beeches Nursery
Ashdon
Nr Saffron Walden
Essex CB10 2HB
www.beechesnursery.co.uk

NCCPG *Agapanthus*
Bicton College of Agriculture
East Budleigh
Budleigh Salterton
Devon EX9 7BY
www.bicton.ac.uk

The Beth Chatto Gardens
Elmstead Market
Colchester
Essex CO7 7DB
www.bethchatto.co.uk

Bressingham Gardens
Bressingham
Diss
Norfolk IP2 2AB
www.bressinghamgardens.com

Dick Fulcher
Pine Cottage Plants
Fourways
Eggesford
Chulmleigh
Devon EX18 7QZ
Tel. 0044-1769-580076
www.pcplants.co.uk
NCCPG National Plant
Collection, *Agapanthus* nursery and a limited assortment
of unusual trees, shrubs and
perennials.

**Royal Horticultural Society
Garden, Wisley**
Woking
Surrey GU23 6QB
www.rhs.org.uk/gardens/wisley

France

Pépinière de L'Île
Charles & Laurence Blasco
Keranroux
22870 Île de Bréhat
(Bretagne)
Tel. and fax 0033-2-96 20 03 84
charlesblasco@aol.com

Germany

Eta Zincke
Agapanthusfreunde
Tel. 0049-30-609 744 09
www.Agapanthus.info

New Zealand

Agapanthus Direct
www.agapanthusdirect.com

Australia

Lambly Nursery
Burnside
Lesters Road
Ascot
Victoria 3364
www.lambley.com

Trevor Nottle
Walnut Hill
Crafers

United States of America

Heronswood Nursery
228th Street
Kingston WA 98 346
www.heronswood.com

Magnolia Gardens Nursery
1980 Bowler Road Waller
Texas 77484
www.magnoliagardensnursery.com

Monterey Bay Nursery
www.montereybaynsy.com

Plant Delights Nursery
9241 Sauls Road
Raleigh NC 27603
www.plantdelights.com

San Marcos Growers
125 South Marcos Road
Santa Barbara CA 9311
www.smgrowers.com

TyTy Agapanthus Nursery
www.tytyga.com

Japan

Komoriya Nursery LTD
1196 Ohkido-cho Chiba-city
Chiba 267-0057
Tel. 81-43-294-4387
Fax 81-43-294-8504

Words of Gratitude

Heard at a garden fair: "I already have a blue and a white *Agapanthus*, now I want a pink one." What do garden lovers really know about these beautiful plants? Nothing at all.
There is a giant gap between experts and laymen, and between specialists and garden lovers.
This book tries to bridge both groups so everyone can enjoy the beautiful *Agapanthus*.
Many thanks to Wim Snoeijer. This book is based on his manuscript and he made order out of chaos thanks to his research and enthusiasm.

Thank you Kees and Catharina Duivenvoorde for all the hospitality, enthusiastic information and clarifications about *Agapanthus*.
Thank you Ignace van Doorslaer for sharing your knowledge and Dick Fulcher for answering my questions.
Wim van der Poel, Chairman of the Publication Committee for The Royal Boskoop Horticultural Society, the RBHS and the board of the RBHS for making this publication possible and for their trust in me.

Photographic Acknowledgements

Wim Snoeijer
Cover and pages 16; 17, top left and bottom right; 19; 23, right; 24; 30; 31, bottom left; 32, center left and bottom, first and fourth from left; 33, right; 35, left; 46; 47; 51; 52, center and right; 53–55; 56, center and right; 57; 58, left; 59–63; 65–82; 85–89; stamps pages 11 and 48 from the collection of Wim Snoeijer.

Hanneke van Dijk and George M. Otter
Pages 2; 6; 13; 21; 22; 23, left; 25–28; 31, top and below right; 32, top, center right and bottom, second and third from left; 33, left; 34; 36, bottom; 37–43; 52, left; 56, left; 58, right; 64; 83; 84; 94.

Kees Duivenvoorde
Pages 17, top right; 35; 36, top and center.

Page 8 courtesy the Library, National Herbarium, Leiden.

Taking *Agapanthus* 'White Heaven' home after enjoying a visit to the Dutch *Agapanthus* Days

Index

Page numbers printed in **boldface** refer to photographs in the text.